ARABIA

SAND · SEA · SKY

for Fawzia

ARABIA

SAND · SEA · SKY

MICHAEL McKINNON

BBC BOOKS

Contents

Published by BBC Books,
a division of BBC Enterprises Limited,
Woodlands, 80 Wood Lane,
London W12 0TT

First published 1990
© Michael McKinnon 1990

ISBN 0 563 36106 9

Designed by Elaine Partington
Map by Line & Line

Set in 12/13½ Garamond
Printed and bound in Great Britain by
Butler & Tanner Ltd, Frome, Somerset
Colour separations by Technik Ltd,
Berkhamsted
Jacket printed by Belmont Press Ltd,
Northampton

grasslands, juniper forests, lichens, woodlands; relict wildlife surviving the drying of the land; Arabian leopard; the high mountains, foothill valleys and links with African wildlife; freshwater fish and amphibians as survivors from a time when rivers flowed; adaptations to the contraction of habitat.

Acknowledgements

This book has been written in the course of the production of the television series of the same title. In consequence it incorporates the work of the many people whose insights have informed the films. The story of Arabian wildlife is only now emerging so that, in addition to the specialized data available in the scientific literature, much valuable information was gathered through conversations with a wide variety of both specialist and amateur enthusiasts.

Professor Wilhelm Buttiker, Dr John Grainger and Dr Peter Vine have been the principal advisors, and without their enthusiasm and great knowledge of the complex ecological linkages in this unfolding story, neither the book nor the films would have their present shape. Peter Vine not only contributed his great knowledge of the Red Sea but made a substantial contribution to the writing of this book.

It was our great fortune that, coinciding with the start of production in 1987, the Saudi Arabian Government established the National Commission of Wildlife Conservation and Development (NCWCD). Within a short period, some 70 sites had been recommended for various degrees of wildlife protection and the activity of scientists from many disciplines was coordinated through the NCWCD in Riyadh. Wildlife conferences, expert committees and innumerable field studies have since that time generated a large body of information. It was due to the generosity of Dr Abdulaziz Abuzinada, the NCWCD Director, that we were given access to much of this research and, crucial to our success, scientists integrated their research and observation programmes with our needs to film specific behaviour.

To mention but a few of the NCWCD scientists whose assistance was invaluable: Abdul Rahman Khojah, Dr Iyad Nader, Phillipe Gaucher, Dr Hany Tatwany, Dr Chris Thouless, Dr Silvan Biquand, Dr Khushal Habibi, Mohammed Sulayem, Mohammed Shobrak, Attia Zahrani, Dr Graham

Child, Othman Llewellyn, Dr Jacque Flamand, Jean Francois Asmode, Peter Symens the Belgian ornithologist who helped throughout the filming with his deep understanding of Arabian ornithology, and Bruno Pambour who provided unique photographs.

Further valuable advice was gathered from Dr Dirar Hassan Nasr of the Institute of Oceanography, Port Sudan, Dr Shawkhat Chowdry, Michael Jennings, Sheila Collenette and Dr Roger Webster. The 11 volumes of *Fauna of Saudi Arabia*, published by The Meteorology and Environmental Protection Administration (MEPA), deepened our understanding of a wide variety of subjects.

Many advisors were not scientists but nevertheless have a deep know-ledge of the peninsula's wildlife: Arthur Stagg has published extensive checklists of the Asir and Riyadh regions and led us many times to key locations. Joy MacGregor and the Desert Ramblers Organization assisted in locating some sites.

In many ways, natural history films are cameramen's films; John Bulmer, Peter Scoones, Tony Bomford and Richard Rosenthal consistently produced wonderful images, often while living and working in difficult conditions. John Hackney, the series film editor with a background in feature films, did much to tighten the narrative of the stories with his sure sense of pacing and so also influenced this book. Organization at the production base in London was fastidiously run by David South as the Managing Executive ably assisted by Samantha Musgrave.

Mohamed Al Edrisi, Associate Producer of the films, performed logistical miracles which allowed us greatly to extend both our region of travel and potential subjects, including the transformation of a request to film in the Rub al-Khali into a 3000-kilometre journey during which we produced the most remarkable images of the series.

I would particularly like to thank the Mobil Corporation, Saudi Aramco and Saudi Basic Industries Corporation (SABIC) for supporting the pro-duction of the series and Mr John R. Hayes for his commitment and dedication to many aspects of the productions from its inception.

Sheila Ableman and Susan Martineau at BBC Books brought both enthusiasm and editorial skill. John Martin coordinated the production of the book and Elaine Partington designed it. Miranda MacQuitty provided valuable research support for both book and films and I would like to thank Paula Casey for her thoughtful editorial assistance on early drafts of the book.

Most of all, I thank my wife, Dr Fawzia Al Sayegh, for stirring an enthusiasm for Arabia nearly 17 years ago and our three children, Rakan, Sarah and Faris, for their patience during my long absences abroad.

7

Preface

A*rabia: Sand, Sea, Sky* has been written with two purposes in mind: as a text which expands upon ideas presented in the television films, and to fill the need for a book which takes a broad overview on Arabia's natural history. While researching for the films, I found many detailed scientific papers but no work which encompassed and linked geological formation, geography and climatic change to the behaviour and evolution of Arabian wildlife.

It became clear that far from being a land of timeless, unchanging deserts, Arabia had undergone dramatic transformations in recent millennia and, in order to understand the wildlife ecology of the present, one must look to the dynamic forces that have shaped the land; to the ebb and flow of climatic change; the ways that changing sea-levels exposed and submerged land bridges so determining migratory pathways; to the rhythms of migration and the expansion and contraction of habitats. It is also apparent that the ecology of the region has now entered a new phase of rapid change under the impact of modernization.

I was intrigued to learn that as recently as 10 000 years ago the Arabian Gulf did not exist, there were no corals in the Red Sea and that the juniper forests extended over the entire 1 200 miles of the Sarawat mountain system. Rock paintings of buffalo and recently discovered fossil bones of rhinoceros gave further indications of a recent verdant past, as did the following description of Wadi al Afal, found in a Greek text written in the second century BC by Agatharchides of Cnidus:

> ... there is a well-watered plain which, because of the streams that flow through it everywhere, grows dog's tooth grass, lucerne and also lotus the height of a man. Because of the abundance and excellence of the pasturage it not only supports flocks and herds of all sorts of unspeakably great numbers

but also wild camels and, in addition antelope and gazelles. In response to the abundance of animals which breed there, crowds of lions, wolves and leopards gather from the desert. Against these the herdsmen are compelled to fight day and night in defence of their flocks.

On the Erythraean Sea

Wadi al Afal lies to the east of the Gulf of Aqaba and is today a dry, barren wadi supporting little life; the Red Sea contains one of the most extensive coral-reef systems on earth and the juniper forests survive only on the highest slopes of the Asir mountains. Much of this contraction of the forests must have taken place since the time of Agatharchides for he portrays it in the following way:

After these people are those called Carbae and after them the Sabaeans who are the most populous of the Arab peoples. They inhabit the region called Eudaemon Arabia (Fortunate Arabia) which bears most of the products considered valuable by us. It also supports herds of animals of all kinds in untold abundance. A natural sweet smell pervades the whole country because almost all plants which are pre-eminent for their fragrance grow unceasingly. Along the coast grows the plant called balsam and cassia and another kind of herb which has a peculiar character. When fresh it gives great pleasure to the eyes, but when it has aged, it quickly fades. In the interior there are dense forests in which there are large frankincense and myrrh trees and in addition palm trees, calamus, and cinnamon trees and others which have a fragrance similar to these. It is not possible to enumerate the peculiarities and characteristics of each because of the amount and overwhelming impact of the combined fragrance from all the trees. For the fragrance appears as something divine and greater than the power of speech to describe as it strikes and stimulates the senses of everyone. As for persons sailing along the coast, although they are far from land, that does not prevent them from sharing this kind of pleasure for in summer, when there is an offshore breeze, it happens that the fragrance which is given off by the myrrh and other such trees reaches the nearby parts of the sea. The case is not as in our countries where the aromatics, having been stored, have a stale quality but, as its power is fresh and in full bloom, it penetrates to the most delicate parts of the senses. For when the breeze carries away the exhalations of the most fragrant trees, a mixture of the noblest perfumes falls on persons sailing towards the coast which is pleasant and powerful as well as healthful and unique since the fruit has not been cut into pieces and lost its peculiar perfection nor has it been stored in vessels of another substance; but it is at its peak of freshness and its divine nature maintains its shoot unblemished so that individuals, who partake of its special quality, think that they have enjoyed the mythical ambrosia because they are unable to discover another appellation that is appropriate to the extraordinary character of is fragrance.

9

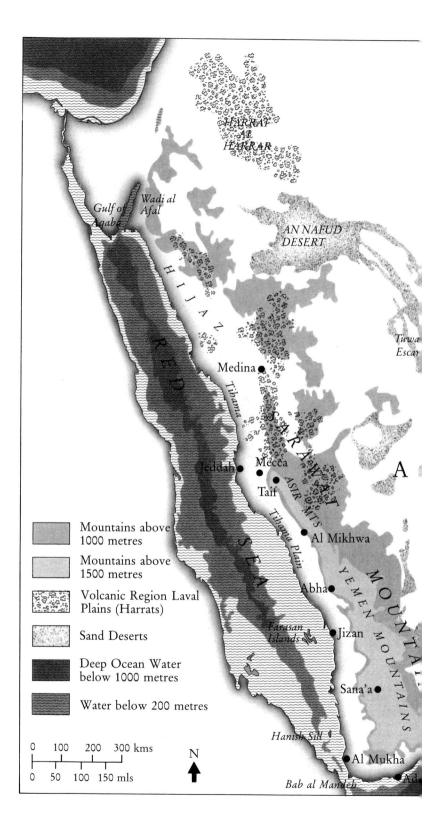

HARRAT
AL
HARRAR

Wadi al
Afal

Gulf of
Aqaba

AN NAFUD
DESERT

H
I
J
A
Z

R
E
D

Tuwa
Escar

Medina

Tihama

SARAWAT

Jeddah   Mecca

Taif

ASIR MTS

A

Tihama Plain

Al Mikhwa

S
E
A

Abha

YEMEN MOUNTAINS

M
O
U
N
T
A
I

Farasan
Islands

Jizan

Mountains above
1000 metres

Mountains above
1500 metres

Volcanic Region Laval
Plains (Harrats)

Sand Deserts

Deep Ocean Water
below 1000 metres

Water below 200 metres

Sana'a

Hanish Sill

0   100   200   300 kms

0   50   100   150 mls

N

Al Mukha

Bab al Mandeb

Ada

Map of Arabia

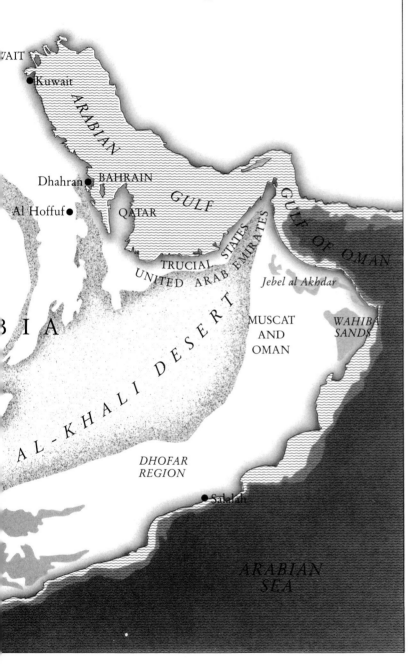

WAIT

• Kuwait

ARABIAN

Dhahran • BAHRAIN

Al Hoffuf •

QATAR

GULF

BIA

TRUCIAL STATES

UNITED ARAB EMIRATES

GULF OF OMAN

Jebel al Akhdar

MUSCAT
AND
OMAN

WAHIBA
SANDS

AL-KHALI DESERT

DHOFAR
REGION

• Salalah

ARABIAN
SEA

Since that ancient time the land of Arabia has continued to dry out, the forests have contracted and much of the remnant wildlife survives only in isolated communities. However, marine life has flourished and the Red Sea has one of the largest and healthiest reef systems on earth. The story of Arabian wildlife is one of continual flux and change, it is a story which began 35 million years ago.

For most of the earth's history the land which we know today as Arabia did not exist as a separate entity but was part of the African continent. Thirty-five million years ago, a great rift in the earth's crust caused Arabia to break away and drift slowly to the east. Eventually this floating plate pressed against Asia and began to wedge itself underneath the lip of the eastern landmass forcing up the Turkish and Iranian mountains. In its wake it created a depression which was later to become the Red Sea. The western margin of the plate was raised by this tilting and at the land's edge a sheer wall was exposed which today rises to 13 000 feet in the south and extends for 1200 miles from Yemen to the Gulf of Aqaba. These violent earth movements moulded the face of Arabia into a peninsula, surrounded on three sides by sea and cut off along its fourth boundary by a vast desert landscape. Arabia also occupies a pivotal position between Africa, Asia and European lands and lies at the centre of the world's largest desert system which runs from Morocco to China. Each of these factors has played an important role in determining the wildlife that we see today.

In order to understand the present ecological conditions and the surviving wildlife in the peninsula, it helps to first imagine how Arabia and its surrounding seas appeared 12 000 years ago, at the end of the last ice age. At that time much of Arabia was covered with verdant grass steppes and savannah plains and must have looked like Africa's Serengeti does today. Arabia's grazing wildlife included buffalo, ostrich, gazelle and oryx, all preyed upon by carnivores such as lion, leopard and cheetah. The mountain areas of the Sarawat escarpment which border the Red Sea to the west, were covered by a continuous belt of juniper which linked the forests of the eastern Mediterranean to the tropical regions of the Ethiopian highlands.

To the south, the Red Sea was closed in, its water level 300 feet lower than today. Animal life was able to move freely across the land bridge between the forest systems of Arabia and Ethiopia. The sea was also colder and much more saline: so much so that reef-building corals were unable to survive and the diverse reef-life which now inhabits this tropical sea did not exist. However, temperatures began to rise about 10 000 years ago and the great masses of water trapped in the polar ice-caps began to melt. Global sea-levels rose and a new cycle of life began as waters from the Indian

Ocean poured back into the Red Sea and flooded over eastern Arabia, giving the Arabian Gulf its present shape.

As snow melted on the Turkish mountains, an immense volume of water poured down into the Tigris and Euphrates rivers causing the legendary deluge described both in the Book of Genesis and the Holy Koran. But further south the Arabian rivers began to dry out and both people and wildlife retreated to oases, shrinking water-courses and to the cooler, moister mountain slopes. Fertile regions continued to contract and indeed are still doing so. The result is that much of Arabia's surviving wildlife is to be found today in isolated locations of endemism. These remaining communities are often confined to a single valley or freshwater pond where conditions have remained relatively stable despite this dramatic shrinkage of habitat.

The drying of the land turned the verdant plains into formidable deserts and it was only the most robust species, capable of evolving strategies to combat this persistent process of drying, that survived. In the mountains many species were able to migrate upwards, colonizing higher ground, escaping the increasing hardships of life in the expanding deserts. It is principally there, in remnant woodlands, that most of Arabia's unique species are still to be found. These contracted habitats can be regarded today as seed-beds of the future, poised to take advantage of any upturn in climatic conditions should rainfall once again increase and temperatures fall. If preserved, they will expand, colonizing more extensive areas, perhaps once more linking up with other similar communities.

When oil was discovered in Arabia, some 60 years ago, few people could have foreseen the astonishing new cycle of change which was about to commence or the profound effects it would have on Arabia's human and natural history. In this brief period there is no part of the vast Arabian peninsula that has not been affected by the consequences of wealth flowing from oil. New road systems have linked the most remote regions to urban centres. Only the great sand deserts have remained relatively isolated but, even there, four-wheel drive vehicles are able to transport livestock, water and fodder to environments previously only accessible to wildlife. Subsidies for feed and animals have brought great security and prosperity to people living in the traditional ways but have also led to an enormous increase in livestock numbers, to such an extent that the impact on the desert has been severe and much of the peninsula's plant life has been heavily over-grazed. Today, the preservation of rangeland and mountain habitats is the most important ecological issue confronting the people of the Arabian peninsula.

Sophisticated drilling techniques have tapped vast quantities of water trapped deep within the rocks, which now support cities, villages and large-

13

scale agricultural projects. The new vegetation and ready availability of water have been particularly beneficial to many bird species both resident and migrant, but the expansion of agriculture has also displaced much native wildlife and disturbed the ecological balance. Recent scientific studies are only now revealing the delicate balance of rangeland ecology and the extent of Arabia's unique botanical heritage. In recent years more than 100 sites have been designated for varying degrees of wildlife protection. It is in these areas, where grazing is prevented by careful management, that the case for conservation has been most clearly demonstrated and proved. Such locations are frequently the sole remaining habitats where the full diversity of native plant and animal life can be found. Enriched by new growth, the protected areas have become secure havens where Arabia's threatened wildlife is being revived. Despite anti-hunting laws a serious decline of the larger animals continues, but ambitious programmes of captive breeding and re-introduction for oryx, gazelle and bustard are helping to stem the tide. However, re-introduction programmes depend upon changes of attitudes by local people and have been most successful when accompanied by extensive public educational campaigns.

In both this book and the associated film series we attempt to provide a broad summary of the current understanding of Arabia's unique natural history. In doing so it is hoped that awareness of the fragility of the peninsula's ecosystems will be more widely recognized. So much of Arabian wildlife is sustained in delicately balanced ecological systems that without the scientific understanding which is now emerging, it has in the past been virtually impossible to assess the environmental consequences of modern developments. Changes have occurred with such speed that much wildlife has been displaced and many animals have come perilously close to extinction. Modernization increasingly makes such heavy demands upon nature that it is hard to over-estimate the vital importance of current conservation programmes. The challenge today is to balance those demands with the sensitive needs of diverse and vulnerable ecologies. The destiny of wildlife and ultimately human life in Arabia will be determined by the success with which botanical abundance and variety is preserved.

1

The
Making
of
Arabia

There are few places on this planet where the geological past is more apparent, or more significant to the present age, than in Arabia. The cataclysmic force of the plates of the earth's crust grinding against each other, twisting and tilting rock layers, and creating steep mountains, can easily be imagined from the exposed, wind-worn and sand-scoured rock strata in many parts of the peninsula. From the Jordan Valley in the north to the soaring peaks of Oman's mountain ranges in the south-east, or the jagged heights of the Asir in the south-west, the evidence of previous earth movements is there for all to see. The barely perceptible widening of the Red Sea, continuing at a rate of a few centimetres per year, is also evidence that continental drift and ocean development, a process which has been happening for over 50 million years, is still going on.

Arabia may be described as a geologist's paradise and indeed many geologists have worn out hammers on its rocks! The reward for their activity has been the unravelling of Arabia's geological past, the discovery of immense underground water wells trapped within the rocks, and the tapping of the world's largest oil reserves which have triggered a dramatic transformation of the peninsula during the past 60 years.

Two hundred million years ago a great super-continent, Gondwana, which included Arabia, lay to the south and was separated by a vast sea from the northern landmass of Laurasia. Around 65 million years ago, Gondwana began to break up and its parts were set adrift from one another on huge floating plates of the earth's crust. Until this period, terrestrial and freshwater life had developed separately, leading to different evolutionary trends, and the emergence of characteristic northern or southern life-forms. At that time Arabia simply did not exist as a separated landmass and its ecology remained part of Gondwana and directly linked to that of Africa. In time Africa itself drifted northwards, and the north-south barrier was eventually broken by the formation of a land bridge linking Afro-Arabia with Laurasia.

Approximately 35 million years ago Arabia began to break from Africa. The split formed a long narrow trench, filled today by the Red Sea. As the Arabian plate separated it drifted north-eastwards, colliding with Asia: the Zagros mountains of Iran and the Hajar range of Oman were the result of this violent clash. As the Arabian plate began to slide under that of Asia the entire Arabian landmass tilted. In the west, the rising edge of the plate formed a 1000-mile wall which can still be seen today in the form of the eroded Sarawat escarpment and the mountains of the Hijaz and Asir, sometimes described as the very spine of Arabia.

The depressed easterly side, pushed down by the Asian plate, slid below sea-level and formed part of a shallow tropical sea, rich in plankton, where sediments accumulated over the millennia and were eventually compressed into rocks. Domes of crystalline salt trapped these carbon deposits and eventually formed the largest oil fields on earth.

The peculiarities of Arabian geology not only trapped oil, but also infinitely greater quantities of water. Cavernous underground reservoirs were filled thousands of years ago when the climate of Arabia was much wetter. A recent study of dried-up lakes in the extremely arid area of Rub al-Khali has shown that two periods of much damper conditions occurred in the relatively recent prehistoric past, from 37 000 to 17 000 years ago and then again, from 10 000 to 5000 years ago. Geologist, Hal McClure, of the Saudi Aramco Oil Company (ARAMCO), who has been investigating these ancient phenomena, believes that there were periods of intense rainfall during those times. Today, rain falling on the western Sarawat escarpment continues to seep eastward into underground water-courses, replenishing hidden water-tables. Because the geological plate rises to over 2000 metres in the west and falls to sea-level at the Arabian Gulf, water trapped in aquifers moves slowly eastwards. Recent studies have shown that water pumped from beneath the ground at Al Hasa oasis in eastern Saudi Arabia fell on the western highlands 40 000 years ago. The current rate of replenishment is, however, quite slow and as more and more of these aquifers are tapped for agricultural development there are increased fears that they may begin to dry up. Despite this, the volume of water contained within Arabia's vast underground water system has been providing a regular output of 18 billion cubic metres per year, almost one third of the annual flow of the River Nile.

Arabia's break with Africa was accompanied by violent movements in the earth's crust and the cleavages at the plates' margins created one of the world's largest volcanic regions. Some of the volcanic cones and craters scattered along the Sarawat mountain range burst through thick layers of

16

basaltic lava laid down at an earlier time, when the rocks were beneath the sea. Evidence for this activity is found throughout the entire length of western Arabia, in the form of extensive volcanic fields or laval plains known as *harrats*. These occur both on the Tihama coastal plain and behind the mountain ridge and they comprise one of the largest regions of volcanic activity on the planet. Among the mountains of Asir and Hijaz, these molten emissions have added height to the peaks, whilst in Yemen up to 1000-metre thick flows of lava have created extensive plateaux. The most recent major eruption in Arabia happened near Medina around 600 years ago. For the most part the volcanic islands of the Red Sea are now dormant, and to a great degree seemingly lifeless except for nesting seabirds. The Red Sea's volcanoes have not all emerged above water however. Some form sea-mounts, with peaks coming within about 50 or 60 metres of the surface, and can only just be reached by scuba divers. Others have been overgrown by corals to form atolls such as those of Sanganeb and Shaab Rumi. Much deeper in the Red Sea however, along the dividing line between the African and Arabian plates, the earth's cauldron of molten lava continues to bubble.

Arabia can be envisaged as an enormous tilted plate, exposing along its western edge an escarpment wall which runs for 1500 kilometres. Behind this mountain wall lies a vast volcanic moonscape of ancient lava flows. In those areas, primarily to the east, where Arabia's tilted plate was inundated by sea the land is covered by limestone. Overlying the ancient sea-bed plateau are extraordinary accumulations of sand forming deserts such as the Rub al-Khali, the largest continuous sand desert on earth, and connected by a thin sliver of a desert, the Dahna, to the northern Arabian Great Nafud desert. It was not always thus. In previous glacial and pluvial periods, the Rub al-Khali supported life, and did so in some abundance. The discovery of remains of hippopotamus and water buffalo in deposits underlying sand-dunes in the south-western Rub al-Khali attest to a more clement era, with a moister climate before the sand-dunes were deposited. Where then did the vast quantities of sand originate? The primary source is crystalline rock abraded by wind, heat and rain along the southern face of the peninsula. Floods, flowing through long eroded valleys known as wadis, carried sand-laden waters to the plains below where they were deposited, rapidly dried by the elements, sorted by a process of winnowing and transported by winds. Other important sources include coastal deposits of sand. When the sea-level was much lower than it is today and large expanses of the Arabian Gulf were above sea-level, sand was blown ashore to create dunes sculpted by ancient winds. A vital factor in the annual movement and redistribution of sand in Arabia still is the *shamal*, or sand-blowing wind, which blows

17

twice a year, during December to January and May to June.

To the west of the Rub al-Khali winds have formed a series of linear dunes shaping giant sand corridors, extending for up to 200 kilometres in length, their summits 100 metres high. In the east of the Rub al-Khali a more complex wind pattern has thrown up great mountains of sand reaching 330 metres or so in height, attesting to the great age of the Rub al-Khali, the history of which is thought to extend back in time at least 2 million years. The Nafud and Dahna deserts also have impressive sand-dunes, some of those in Dahna reaching to 170 metres. The Nafud is renowned for its dramatic crescent-shaped sand-hills whilst those of the Dahna are less regular and more varied in form.

Apart from vast deserts of sand and extensive alluvial gravel flats, residual stone desert plains called regoliths, the result of prolonged weathering, are also found in Arabia. Although there are no permanent rivers in Arabia, heavy rain carries vast quantities of sand and rock down wadis, depositing them across alluvial flood plains. During the last ice age rivers did flow, in some cases reaching the sea. The most recent river system was at Wadi Al Batin which flowed as a continuous water course up to 3000 years ago, but is now mostly clogged by sand. This system's rushing, hard gravel-laden waters cut steep-sided banks through softer limestone, gouging out a distinctive course, eventually dumping a heavy burden out over a huge triangular plain which spreads today across parts of Kuwait and Iraq. Other previously flowing rivers include the Nisah-Sabah wadi system which drained the central Tuwaiq escarpment eastwards across the desert as far as Qatar. A third ancient river system, the Dawasir, once reaching as far as the Gulf region, has created a broad gravel plain, much of which is presently covered by sands of the Rub al-Khali. Numerous other wadi systems, throughout Arabia, have created alluvial plains, and in many cases these have been chosen as sites for agricultural developments.

Along the coastal plains of Arabia salt deserts have been formed by rise and fall of surrounding seas. They are known as *sabkha* (a term derived from the Arabic for a saline flat). Bordering the Arabian Gulf extensive salt flats extend for 322 kilometres and are up to 32 kilometres wide. While they appear to be quite hard, the *sabkha* surface, a congealed cake of crystalline salt, often overlies a soft muddy quagmire of sand, making them dangerous for wheeled vehicles, even those of the four-wheel drive variety! In some areas *sabkha* deserts are a considerable height above sea-level; at Hoffuf in eastern Saudi Arabia for example, they are 150 metres higher than present-day sea-level and are the residue from a previous period of high sea-level. Elevated *sabkhas* are by no means the only evidence we have to prove that the Arabian Gulf once flooded over much of the eastern Arabian plain.

Other features indicating that this occurred include a low-level shell and tube-worm reef and various wave-cut coral cliffs, far inland; together with deltas of previously flowing wadis, existing over 100 metres above present-day sea-levels. Today, these ancient corals litter the extensive plains above the Tuwaiq escarpment in the very centre of Arabia.

The Arabian Gulf is a relatively shallow sea with an average depth of only 35 metres. Even the deepest parts do not exceed 110 metres. Approximately 5 million years ago seas rose up to 150 metres above present levels. The Gulf waters flooded much of low-lying eastern Arabia during this period, and extended north into the delta of the Tigris and Euphrates rivers. Much more recently, during the last ice age, between 70 000 to 10 000 years ago, great quantities of ice trapped in the polar ice caps, resulted in a lowering of sea-level, to about 120 metres below present-day levels. At this time the Arabian Gulf more or less emptied of sea-water and the Tigris and Euphrates rivers extended all the way to the Straits of Hormuz. These lower sea-levels also affected the Red Sea, isolating it from the Indian Ocean (at the Hanish Sill north of the southern straits of Bab al Mandeb). As the Red Sea loses 2 metres of water per year in evaporation this led to a dramatic lowering of sea-level and an increase in salinity. All Red Sea corals and much of their associated marine life died off at this time. Whilst geologists have interpreted the evidence of wave-cut cliff faces on land as confirmation of previously higher sea-levels, so scuba divers often encounter similar phenomena beneath the surface of the Red Sea indicating previously low sea-levels. In some cases these submarine erosional features are as clearly defined as those which we find on land. At the end of the last ice age rising sea-levels brought the rich tropical waters of the Indian Ocean flooding back into the Red Sea and Gulf.

While both the Gulf and Red Sea are fed from the Indian Ocean, they are quite different in character; the Red Sea being long, narrow and deep in contrast to the shorter, broader and shallower Gulf. Along the mid-line of the Red Sea, where a series of 'Deeps' filled with hot brines occur, it reaches as much as 2850 metres deep. Ever since its early formation the Red Sea has been dependent upon an influx of sea-water from either the Mediterranean (Sea of Tethys) or the Indian Ocean. During periods of total or partial isolation sea-levels fell dramatically. In one such period, 10 million years ago, when in-flow from the Mediterranean was greatly restricted, the replenishment rate failed to compensate for evaporative loss causing a dramatic lowering of sea-level and a great increase in salinity. Approximately 5 million years ago geological activity increased, accelerating the widening process and further deepening the Red Sea. At the same time a general tilting of the plates elevated the lands surrounding the northern Red Sea and isolated it from the Mediterranean, whilst to the south, as the Arabian and African plates twisted apart from each other, the Indian Ocean flooded in through the narrow bottle-neck at the Straits of Bab al Mandeb. This was not the end of the story however for sea-levels also fell during periodic ice ages, by as much as 120 metres in the last ice age, and rose during intervening warmer periods. During these periods of isolation waters cooled, salinity rose, and much of the Red Sea's marine life died. We are witnessing a similar phenomenon today in the Dead Sea which once extended down into the Red Sea via the Gulf of Aqaba but is now cut of from it. As the Gulf of Aqaba slowly widens we can expect a channel to appear reconnecting the deep pit of the Dead Sea, presently with water at 400 metres below sea-level, with the Red Sea. At this time, just as happened in the past with the Red Sea, sea-water will pour into the trench, refilling it, flooding parts of the Jordan Valley and creating a coral sea full of fish where today nothing but salt-loving bacteria survive.

In the case of the Red Sea, its most recent reconnection with the Indian Ocean came about around 15 000 years ago, as sea-level once more began to rise, towards the end of the last ice age. It is the view of many biologists that virtually all the Red Sea's present marine life, including its high proportion of endemic species, colonized its reefs after this latest flooding in of sea-water. In both the Red Sea and Arabian Gulf sea-levels have to some extent stabilized during the last 7000 years, with fluctuations of around 2 metres. The Red Sea rift is part of the longest rift system on earth, the Great Rift valley stretching from Mozambique in southern Africa to the Dead Sea. The two plates continue to drift apart at a rate which leads geologists to project that it would take another 200 million years for the Red Sea to reach the dimensions of today's Atlantic Ocean. Indeed, it has been described as 'an ocean in the making' but we have no way of knowing whether the process of drift will continue or whether stability will be reached and the status quo maintained for a much greater period.

As the two plates continue to separate, molten magma is extruded into the long narrow fissure along the mid-line of the Red Sea, filling an ever-widening gap. Photographs taken in these Red Sea deeps indicate the extent of submarine eruptions. Huge flows of lava are rapidly cooled on contact with sea-water, forming bizarre shaped rocks, similar to piles of pillows. Sea-water in the vicinity of these fissures, heated by the volcanic activity, attains much higher temperatures than surface waters, a reversal of the normal relationship of sea-water temperature compared to depth. Average deep sea temperatures approach 22° Centigrade compared with 5° Centigrade at similar depths in the Indian Ocean. Salinity is also affected, reaching around 360 parts per thousand in contrast to normal sea-water which is 36 parts per thousand.

The consistency of the hot muds in the Red Sea formed by the precipitation of valuable salts has been recently investigated by scientists who have found that the muds vary from quite soft in the surface layers 'to a material with the consistency of boot polish' deeper down. It is estimated that these mineral-rich muds could yield at least 60 000 tons of zinc, 10 000 tons of copper, 100 tons of silver and 1.1 tons of gold per year. The great challenge would be to do so without polluting the marine environment.

The geological processes described in this chapter took millions of years to give Arabia its present shape. Such changes not only affected marine life but also influenced the evolution of terrestrial wildlife. As we shall see in the next chapter, the origins and current distribution of Arabian wildlife owe much to this geological record.

———————————

2

The Dawn of Arabian Wildlife

Arabian wildlife owes much to its pivotal location between Africa and Eurasia. To this day the peninsula is one of the most important north-south and east-west migratory pathways for nearly three billion birds. The periodic existence of land bridges, resulting from the rise and fall of the oceans, has brought terrestrial species from the neighbouring zones of Africa and Asia whilst, in the north, wildlife migrations in and out of Arabia have been controlled by climatic factors. Major cycles of climatic change have occurred approximately every 100 000 years. Long periods of cold conditions alternate with periods of global warming. Not only is wildlife directly affected by these climatic variations, but, as we have seen, the changes are also accompanied by major fluctuations in sea-level, dramatically altering the shape of the land and indeed the existence or physical nature of surrounding seas.

Recent studies of eastern Saudi Arabian sedimentary and fossil deposits, dating from 17 to 19 million years ago, have highlighted the importance of land connections resulting from climatic fluctuations. It has been shown, for example, that Arabia was joined by land to south-west Asia 18 million years ago. It is now believed that Arabia thus formed part of a continuous land bridge connecting Africa to Asia. Such land bridges have come into being at various times since then. Indeed, as recently as the last ice age, when the seas were 120 metres below present levels, much of the Arabian Gulf was dry land across which animals could move freely. Simultaneously, Africa was joined to south-western Arabia at the Hanish Sill near the southern end of the Red Sea.

Because of these intermittent links with other landmasses, the predominant feature of Arabia's ecology is one of alternate immigration and isolation. It would be wrong, however, to consider Arabia itself as a single ecological zone for the peninsula is a vast land, the size of Western Europe, containing many different environments, from arid deserts to high, forested mountain peaks. Individual habitats, separated from each other by natural barriers, became centres for the evolution of new, distinctly Arabian life-forms.

Compelling evidence of Arabia's more verdant epochs has recently been discovered among the *sabkha* salt flats at Ad Dabtiyah in eastern Saudi Arabia. The 18-million-year-old remains of an Asian elephant-like mastodon (*Gomphotherium cooperi*), previously known only from deposits in Pakistan, were found along with two species of rhinoceros. Six ruminants, including an ancient form of giraffe, were also discovered together with a new species of hominoid (*Heliopithecus leakeyi*) which appears to be closely similar to an African form from the same period (*Afropithecus turkanensis*). Analysis of this site, and its rich hoard of fossils, has drawn palaeontologists to conclude that the wildlife living around Ad Dabtiyah 17 to 19 million years ago occupied a tropical area of freshwater ponds inhabited by small ancient carp-like fish and surrounded by palm trees and other woodland. It is also clear from such finds that the distribution of Arabian fauna and flora was part of a much more extensive wildlife system which stretched from Africa, through Europe and Asia.

A recent examination of fossil deposits in the United Arab Emirates uncovered remains of elephants, hippopotamus, small carnivores, horses, crocodiles, turtles, freshwater fish and unusually thick ostrich eggshells. This unlikely treasure was discovered in an ancient river-bed, long since dried up, and in an area which today is extremely arid. An ancient relative of the horse, *Hipparion,* was found amongst this hoard of fossils and helped geologists to pin down their age to around eight million years. A single tooth of a macaque-like monkey, the first to be found on the Arabian peninsula, also provided valuable evidence of Arabia's close biological links with Africa. It is of special significance since, although it is the same age as similar finds in Africa, fossil remains of these monkeys in Asia are all younger, pointing to a migratory trend from Africa across Arabia towards Asia. Encouraged by this valuable discovery, the expedition's leading vertebrate palaeontologist, Peter Whybrow from the British Museum, has concluded that the fossils confirm the importance of the Arabian peninsula, and the Middle East in general, as a corridor for animal migrations between Europe, Africa and Asia.

The fossil evidence of Arabia's early mammals demonstrates strong links with Africa, the first indications of immigrations from south-west Asia occurring in the Miocene period (25 to 5 million years ago). During this time, as already explained, Arabia and Africa were joined by a broad land bridge at the southern end of the Red Sea, linking Ethiopia and Yemen.

23

The early fossil record not only proves that Arabia once supported a range of species quite different from those which live there today, but also provides an important basis for our understanding of how present zoogeography has been established.

Among the varied fauna and flora of the Arabian peninsula are found examples of plants and animals which have originated from a variety of areas: (1) the extensive deserts and temperate zones of North Africa, Asia and Europe; (2) tropical East Africa; (3) the Orient: summarized basically as Palaearctic, Ethiopian and Oriental.

Arabia's Palaearctic wildlife is mostly found today among its cooler highland regions, and in the far north of the peninsula, where climatic conditions are as close as possible to those which existed across most of Arabia during previous ice ages. Climatic changes, and principally increased aridity, seem to have been responsible for a 'faunal break' or wave of extinctions during the last ice age. It is clear that extinctions occurred steadily, with four large mammals (warthog, lynx and two species of rhinoceros) disappearing between 70 000 and 40 000 years ago. Three more became extinct between 40 000 and 10 000 years ago – two horse species and the spotted hyena. Between that time and about 100 years ago wild dromedary camel, elephant and hippopotamus have disappeared from Arabia. The last century has seen further extinctions including cheetah, Bubal hartebeest, lion and a species of Red Sea seal. A tantalizing taste of the ancient abundance of now extinct creatures is conveyed by Agatharchides of Cnidus, writing in the second century BC:

> The lions in Arabia are less hairy and bolder. The sheen of their mane is such that the hair on the back of their necks gleams like gold.

> After sailing past the Palm-Grove one encounters near a promontory of the mainland an island which has been named Seal Island from the animals that live on it. For so great a number of these animals frequent these places that observers were amazed. The promontory, which is situated in front of the island, lies below the area called the Rock and Palestine. It is to this region that the Gerrhaeans and Minaeans bring, as is the report, frankincense and other aromatic products from what is called upper Arabia.
>
> *On the Erythraean Sea*

Further evidence of the mammalian record of recent millennia can be found in innumerable carvings on rock faces dating back 7000 years. These forms of rock art indicate the importance of, among other things, ibex and wild oxen to the lives of Arabia's early inhabitants. Also featured are hyenas, camels and ostriches. Whilst a high proportion of Arabia's larger wild mammals have been threatened as a result of hunting and displacement during the past few thousand years, and in particular over the past 100 years, remote areas within Arabia still harbour significant populations of mammals, many of which are uniquely adapted to live in extremely arid environments and these provide an excellent model for demonstrating the predominant affinities of Arabian wildlife, reflecting the proximity and significance of Africa, Europe and Asia.

The wolf (*Canis lupus arabs*), a large, robust creature looking something like an overgrown hairy Alsatian, is a widespread Palaearctic species, once distributed throughout Europe, Asia and North America. In Arabia it is still relatively common and well known to many Bedouin farmers who take measures to protect their animals against its incursions. There are two races present; *pallipes* to the north and the smaller *arabs* to the south. Like the wolf, Arabian foxes also spring from Palaearctic sources. The Arabian fox (*Vulpes vulpes arabica*), largest of the four species of Arabian foxes, is the most commonly seen, often caught in the headlights of cars at night. Like several other mammalian species, it has learnt to benefit from Man's urban developments, frequently feeding at rubbish dumps. Rüppell's sand fox (*Vulpes ruppelli sabaea*) a much more delicate creature, well adapted to live in the desert, and widely distributed throughout Arabia with the exception of the Red Sea coastal plain, is also found in the deserts of northern Africa. Blandford's fox (*vulpes cana*) occurs in the Irano-Indian region and has recently been discovered in several areas of Arabia. An even smaller fox, and probably the most beautiful of the four species, is the fennec fox, *Fennecus zerda* which, like Rüppell's fox, has large ears, but can be easily distinguished by its black-tipped tail. It is extremely well-adjusted to desert life and can exist without drinking water, living on a diet of insects, lizards, rodents and more plant material than most other carnivores, burrowing deep into desert sands to avoid the worst excesses of the sun's heat. This species is also distributed across the deserts of North Africa.

Nocturnal and reclusive honey badgers or ratel (*Mellivora capensis pumilio*) are distinctively patterned in black and white with impressive defence armaments in the form of huge claws and anal glands capable of secreting a foul odour. They are also found in many parts of Africa, the Levant and Asia. The Indian grey mongoose (*Herpestes edwardsi ferrugineus*), on the other hand, most probably arrived by boat from Asia. This attractive, small creature with a long bushy tail is frequently found among palm groves or well-watered agricultural areas, especially in Kuwait, Bahrain and among the eastern oases of Saudi Arabia. It hunts for a variety of food items including scorpions, fish, rodents, birds and carrion. The related white-tailed mongoose (*Ichneumia albicauda*) is larger than the Indian form and is primarily found in the mountainous parts of southern Arabia: elsewhere it occurs in many areas of Africa. Genets (*Genetta felina granti*), sporting slender blotched bodies, short legs, long, bushy, banded tails, small heads and large ears, hunt at night for birds, reptiles, amphibians, small mammals, insects and a variety of fruits and other vegetable matter. Genets as a group are found throughout southern Europe and in much of Africa. The striped hyena (*Hyaena hyaena sultana*) is a relatively large mammal easily distinguishable by a dorsal mane running from head to tail. It emerges under cover of darkness from its daytime caves in search of carrion, reptiles, insects, vegetable matter and even dried bones from which they derive the organic bone-building substance called collagen. In the absence of carrion it has been known to kill large domestic animals such as goats, sheep, horses or even camels. The two Arabian races, a northern *syriaca* and a southern *sultana,* are widely distributed across north Africa, Asia Minor, and as far as India.

Widely distributed too, this time from as far north as Scotland through parts of eastern and southern Europe, Asia and parts of Africa, is the wild cat (*Felis silvestris gordoni*). It has the appearance of a domestic cat but is somewhat larger and bears a shorter black-ringed tail with a dark tip. In Arabia they are principally found in mountain areas. Wild cats in general are nocturnal animals, rarely seen by Man, and efficient predators of birds, reptiles, small mammals and insects. The sand cat (*Felis margarita*), a most graceful creature, unlike the wild cat, is especially adapted to desert life. The soles of its feet are covered by hairs, enabling it to walk rapidly over soft sand without sinking. This species probably feeds on sand skinks and burrowing agamid lizards and appears to be able to live without any source of drinking water. Outside of Arabia it is found in North Africa, probably south-eastern Iraq, parts of Iran, and as far east as Pakistan. The caracal (*Caracal caracal schmitzi*) stands to about 45 centimetres shoulder-height. It has black vertical bars over the eyes and distinctive long ear tufts and, though common, is widely distributed in Arabia, living in caves or rock crevices and hunting birds, mammals, reptiles and amphibians. This species also occurs over most of Africa (except the Sahara and rainforest regions), Sinai and eastwards to the Irano-Indian region.

Leopard and cheetah, typical savannah land creatures, once enjoyed a wide distribution stretching from most of Africa to India. In Arabia, as the climate dried, leopards were forced up into the mountains in search of their prey. Today this emigrant from the plains survives only on Arabia's highest mountains where it has evolved as a distinct Arabian sub-species, smaller than its African ancestor.

Cheetahs (*Acinonyx jubatus venaticus*), on the other hand, are probably extinct now in Arabia, although records of its presence during this century

26

do leave hope that individuals will still be discovered in some remote region of the peninsula.

The Arabian peninsula has been described as 'the heartland of the distribution of the true gazelles' and, whilst affinities with African counterparts do exist, gazelles have occupied Arabia since the dawn of their evolution. There are at present five species living in the peninsula and their isolation has encouraged the development of racial differences, leading in several cases to the raising of sub-species. The Palestine mountain gazelle (*Gazella gazella gazella*), a large, dark-coloured, straight-horned gazelle, lives among mountains along the eastern Mediterranean seaboard, not strictly speaking within the boundaries of Arabia. A more widely distributed sub-species, often referred to as *Gazella gazella arabica* and known locally as *idmi,* is somewhat lighter in colour, exceptionally long-legged and slender-bodied with slightly out-turned horns. It occupies *Acacia* plains, usually around foothills of mountainous regions. A third sub-species of this form, the Muscat gazelle (*Gazella gazella muscatensis*), more robust but smaller and darker than the other two, inhabits the coastal region of northern Oman.

The dorcas gazelle (*Gazella dorcas*) also lives in the western desert of Egypt. Isolation from what is believed to be this original parent stock has led to the development of two distinct sub-species, Isabella dorcas gazelle (*Gazella dorcas isabella*) and the Saudi gazelle (*Gazella dorcas saudiya*). The former lives primarily along the Sudanese Red Sea coast but some individuals are found in Jordan so it might just be regarded as a possible member of the Arabian list. The latter, known locally as *afri,* is the true peninsula form. It is recognizable by the almost total absence of a flank stripe (contrasting with the Isabella dorcas), a light face crowned by two long straight horns, long ears and a short tail. The Saudi gazelle, like its cousins, displays a rapid turn of speed when alarmed, literally bounding across the desert in elegant flight.

The Arabian sand gazelle or *rhim* (*Gazella subgutturosa marica*) has relatives in Iraq, parts of the USSR, Iran and even Mongolia. Its colouration, perfectly matching the sandy desert, makes it almost invisible on the landscape, even when one is quite close to crouched or stationary animals. The Farasan island gazelle has quite recently been recognized as the true form of *Gazella arabica*. It is the single Arabian gazelle which most closely resembles *Gazella gazella,* being larger than other Arabian species, reddish-brown in colour, and with a poorly defined dark flank stripe. Queen of Sheba's gazelle (*Gazella bilkis*) known as the Yemen mountain gazelle, is also dark in colour but bears a well-defined flank stripe, and only occurs in the mountains of North Yemen (and possibly south-eastern Saudi Arabia).

The Arabian oryx (*Oryx leucoryx*) is the only Arabian member of the antelope family. Extinct in the wild, it has now been re-introduced following a massive rescue operation. The last wild oryx are believed to have been killed in Saudi Arabia in 1969, and in Oman in 1972. It is one of the few Arabian indigenous species, clearly evolving as such within Arabia, and once extending its range into the deserts of Syria and Iraq, as well as throughout the desert plains of the peninsula proper. The nubian ibex (*Capra ibex nubiana*), resembling a rather stout goat, the male of which possesses long curved horns, lives among steep, craggy mountains, in terrain where few other large mammals can survive. Despite a serious depletion in numbers it does still occur in some remote areas of Arabia along the Sarawat, and in the Omani mountains. Plentiful in prehistoric times, it is depicted in many rock carvings from both the Palaeolithic and Neolithic periods. Wild goat (*Capra aegagrus*), related to the ibex, and recognizable by the scimitar-like long curved horns of the adult male, presently ranges from the Greek islands throughout Asia Minor, with a few isolated herds surviving in Oman. It is also present in Iran and Pakistan, and it has been suggested that the Arabian population stems from the time of Arabia's ancient land bridge with Iran, across the area of the Gulf. There are other suggestions that wild goats were actually introduced by Man into Arabia.

The Arabian tahr (*Hemitragus jayakari*), like the Arabian oryx, is indigenous to Arabia, living today in the mountains of Oman, although related species occur in India. Its Latin name, *Hemitragus,* means half-goat, and indeed it is quite difficult to distinguish young tahr from goats.

Cape hare (*Lepus capensis*) is well-adapted for life in desert areas with its large ears which help to dissipate heat, and is among the most frequently seen small mammal in the Arabian desert, forming a regular part of the Bedouin diet who still hunt them with saluki dogs.

A species whose origin is Indian rather than African or northern is the Indian crested porcupine (*Hystrix indica*). It is also the largest Arabian rodent, measuring about 80 centimetres when fully grown. Rarely seen by Man, this nocturnal creature, inhabiting burrows and small caves in the daytime, emerges at night to feed on vegetable material and frequently damages crops. It is a favoured food of the Bedouin.

Arabian deserts and steppelands would not be the same without jerboas, small agile rodents with exceedingly long back legs on which they hop, using their long tails for extra balance. The Euphrates jerboa (*Allactaga euphratica*) lives in the northern parts of the peninsula whilst the lesser jerboa (*Jaculus jaculus*) is common in most parts of Arabia's sandy deserts. Several species of mice and rats are also to be found in Arabia, some of which are natural to the area, whilst others, like the Norway rat (*Rattus norvegicus*), the house rat (*Rattus rattus*), and the house mouse (*Mus musculus*) have certainly been introduced inadvertently by Man through seaports all around the peninsula. Among the small rodents, the Indian gerbil or antelope rat (*Tatera indica*) originated in Asia and has spread westwards through Iran to Iraq and Syria, as far as Kuwait. It is a water-dependent species, primarily found in agricultural areas.

Before leaving the topic of Arabia's small rodents mention should also be made of other gerbils and jirds such as Sundevall's jird (*Meriones crassus*), the Libyan jird (*Meriones libycus*) and Cheesman's gerbil (*Gerbillus cheesmani*). All these forms appear to owe their origins to ancestors from the north and east, rather than from Africa. The only Arabian endemic rodent is the king jird (*Meriones rex*) which lives in high altitudes of the Asir (from 1350 to 2200 metres). It occupies well-organized burrows, compartmentalized into food storage chambers and a deeper nest chamber, emerging in the evening to feed on shoots and among bushes, and sometimes on crops. Communication between individuals underground is achieved by banging feet against the floor of the burrow.

The black hedgehog, also known as Brandt's hedgehog (*Paraechinus hypomelas*), is thought to have arrived from Iran. Still inhabiting parts of western Arabia and the high mountains of Oman and Yemen, it has also been found on Jebel Hafit in the United Arab Emirates. By contrast, the Ethiopian hedgehog (*Paraechinus aethiopicus*) is much more widespread and is able to withstand extremely arid conditions. A third species, the long-eared hedgehog (*Hemiechinus auritus*), has a primarily northern distribution, including Kuwait, but not penetrating far into the peninsula proper. The Indian house shrew (*Suncus murinus*), an insect-eater superficially resembling a rodent but easily distinguished by a long pointed snout and short fur, is one of Man's messmates and has been introduced to Arabia from Asia. Since this shrew usually occurs close to seaports it is reasonable to presume that it has been carried on board ships which have for long plied trade routes between India and Arabia.

Arabian ancestry of the hamadryas baboon (*Papio hamadryas*) has stirred considerable debate even though its ancient origins, well documented by fossil finds in Africa, can be traced back to the Upper Miocene period. The hamadryas baboon is found in the horn of Africa, from south Sudan to Somalia, and along the west coast of the Arabian peninsula. Whilst the African population appears to be under severe threat of extinction, the Arabian population flourishes to the point of causing local disquiet and demands for their control. Although the hamadryas is the only living primate in Arabia, others lived here millions of years ago, as revealed by recent fossil finds. There is no doubt that the original ancestor came from Africa, possibly a shared ancestor with the anubis baboon (*Papio anubis*)

29

which is presently found on East Africa's savannah, and with which the hamadryas shares many features. However, it is quite possible that the hamadryas actually evolved as a distinct species in Arabia. The location of hamadryas baboons on both sides of the southern Red Sea is possibly explained by the fact that they were carried on board trading vessels which have regularly crossed these waters for at least 5000 years. The hamadryas baboon was the sacred baboon of the ancient Egyptians and was certainly transported on their vessels. The question remains, however, did they originate in Arabia and colonize East Africa, or was it the other way around? One piece of evidence supporting the probability that it is actually an African species, introduced into Arabia, is its absence from the Oman mountains, a habitat which would appear to be as suitable for occupation as its present base in the Yemen and the Sarawat mountain range.

> The animals called 'dog-heads' are similar to malformed men as far as their bodies are concerned, and they make manlike whimpering sounds with their voices. These animals are very wild and completely untamable. They have a rather fierce appearance because of their brows. Their females have the peculiarity of bearing their womb outside of their body all the time.
>
> *On the Erythraean Sea,* Agatharchides of Cnidus
> (second century BC)

The distribution pattern of the baboon is also reflected among reptiles. No tropical reptiles are found today among the Oman mountains despite the fact that local climatic conditions would appear to be no less suitable for them than those in the Yemen. It is thus clear that although tropical species may have existed in the Oman mountains during the Tertiary period (70 million to 4 million years ago), the onset of colder weather in this region during the subsequent Pleistocene period, led to these being replaced there by species better adapted to local conditions. Given this context, the absence of hamadryas baboons might not be taken as such firm evidence for an African origin of the species.

Scientists studying hamadryas baboons in Arabia have identified significant behavioural differences between those living on the peninsula and those in Ethiopia. The question of where precisely they evolved as a distinct species remains to be answered. It is possible that further light may be thrown on this issue by studies on fossils found in caves among the Omani mountains.

Arabia's reptiles also provide strong evidence of its zoogeographical links with Africa, Europe and Asia. Approximately one quarter of the peninsula's reptile genera are Afro-tropical. This group of species, characterized by a dependence upon humid conditions, is entirely confined to south-west Arabia and is not found elsewhere in Asia. Of the remainder, almost half are classified as Saharo-Sindian element species able to traverse arid areas and characteristically displaying a strong east-west distributional range within the Old World arid belt. Arabia's ancient links with its surrounding regions is further emphasized by the fact that there are no endemic reptilian genera in Arabia.

Desert geckos in the genus *Stenodactylus,* including such forms as Slevin's ground gecko (*S. sleveni*), have their evolutionary centre in southern Arabia. We know from blood analysis comparing related species that their ancestors have lived in Arabia since the early Tertiary period, about 60 million years ago.

Pristurus is a genus of rock gecko which is distributed from Somalia to southern Iran, irrespective of sea or desert barriers, but always near the coast. The densest populations of this genus occur on either side of the Gulf of Aden. The genus of spiny-tailed lizards, *Uromastyx,* on the other hand, has entered Arabia from the east. Its closest relative is a south-east Asian genus *Leiolepis* whilst its most primitive extant member, *Uromastyx wickii,* lives in Pakistan. Again, blood analysis data supports this view and suggests that members of the primitive eastern group invaded Arabia at the time of the close of the Tethys Sea (Mediterranean) about 18 million years ago. Geographic isolation since then has led to the development of separate species.

A genus of agamid lizards known as *Stellio,* includes two Arabian forms, *Stellio adramitana* and *Stellio yemenensis.* The genus itself is most definitely of central Asian origin. What is most interesting however is that there are five species within the genus living in East Africa, from Ethiopia and Somalia, south to Natal. Apart from being present in Mediterranean Egypt, *Stellio* is absent from North Africa or north Arabia. It seems most likely therefore that the ancient route by which the genus spread was across the Gulf, from Iran to Arabia, and from Yemen to Africa, across the ancient land bridge, prior to rifting. Separation of African and Arabian populations following the drift apart of the two landmasses, led to speciation. It may be however that subsequent land connections, caused by sea-level lowering, led to more recent spread of one species.

The genus of viperid snakes known as *Echis,* is both well known and well distributed. The genus is believed to be related to the African vipers, and includes three representatives living in Arabia; Burton's carpet viper (*E.coloratus*), Sochurch carpet viper (*E.carinatus*), and saw-scaled viper (*E.pyramidum*). The former lives around both coasts of the Red Sea, from northern Sudan to southern Yemen with isolated populations occurring near Riyadh and in the Oman mountains. *E.carinatus* is an eastern species

31

whose only Arabian population exists in the Oman region, whilst *E.pyr-amidum* is an African species. As such it shares with many other African forms a typically restricted Arabian distribution, confined to the south-west of the peninsula, where conditions are more humid.

The cobra genus, *Naja,* and the chameleon (*Chamaeleo*) are both derived from Ethiopia, and have spread as far as India. There are however huge gaps in their distribution, being absent from south-west Iran to Baluchistan. In Arabia they are confined to mountainous areas in the south-west, repeating the trend described for many other Afro-tropical immigrants to Arabia. Like many of these African forms they are dependent on finding moist conditions and it is hardly surprising therefore that they do not occur throughout large tracts of the Middle East. Their presence in India does, however, suggest that a moist environment existed for their journey eastwards, and we know that such conditions occurred across much of southern Arabia during the middle Miocene, around 18 million years ago. It would thus appear that their migration may have followed the same route as the spiny lizard, *Uromastyx,* but in the reverse direction.

Worm-lizards are related to both lizards and snakes, and are limbless with a concentrically-grooved cylindrical body. Both Arabian worm-lizards, *Diplometopon zarudnyi* and *Leptotyphlops macrorhyus,* are found in Mesopotamia and down the Gulf coast to Oman, and *Agamodon arabicus* in Yemen. Two other members of this family occur in Somalia. Based on these separate and unconventional distribution patterns it has been concluded that these two reptile groups are relicts of a very ancient and now widely extinct Afro-Arabian reptile fauna.

It is clear from these and indeed many other examples that tropical species have entered south-west Arabia, after its split from Africa, by means of land bridges created by the lowering of sea-level during ice ages. No doubt some terrestrial species also crossed the marine divide by 'rafting' (clinging to floating material). In the case of the reptiles, however, there are few if any examples of species which travelled in this way. Certainly, the presence of seven Somalian/Eritrean snakes in south-west Arabia supports the theory of a land bridge rather than rafting since these are notoriously poor colonizers of oceanic islands.

Africa's indigenous fauna had evolved in conditions of moderately moist to wet conditions. Nearly all were dependent upon a reasonable supply of water. Despite climatic shifts over thousands of years, it now seems unlikely that the savannah conditions required for many African tropical species have ever provided a continuous north-south corridor through north-east Africa during the past 4 million or so years. Even in the last great glacial period which reached its zenith 18 million years ago, conditions did not

Previous page: The jigsaw-like fit of the Arabian and African coastlines in the southern Red Sea reflects the time when the two landmasses were joined together. Water from the Indian Ocean (on the right of the picture) pours into the Red Sea to renew both marine life and water lost through evaporation.

The vast basaltic stone deserts of western Arabia are the residue of Arabia's long volcanic history which commenced 50 million years ago, when Arabia started to slide away from Africa, and continued intermittently until quite recent times. Covered by basalt rocks which were spewed out of immense volcanoes, these regions are known as harrats. Harrat al Harrah *(above) covers an area of 55 000 square kilometres.*

The immense sedimentary plain of central Arabia is divided by the 1200-kilometre-long wall of the Tuwaiq escarpment (right). The meandering escarpment face with its high caves and rock pools has long been a haven for ibex, desert owls, eagles, wolves, endemic fish and much other desert wildlife.

The Tihama coastal plain bordering the
Red Sea displays many forms of volcanic
activity such as the two large volcanic
domes (left). Much of the region's
wildlife and vegetation has strong
affinities with Africa, like Adenium
obesum which is frequently found in
clusters of basalt rocks or in the midst
of lava flows (left). Some Adenium
exhibit their pink flowers (above) even
when they are not in leaf.

Above: the desert eagle owl prefers the wild desert mountains of northern Arabia with their myriad cliffs, crags and rocky outcrops. It nests on ledges or crevices and occasionally even in wells. Its range extends right across the North African desert region.

Right: The Abyssinian roller is found along the wild Tihama coastal region that borders the Red Sea where the dry, cultivated tree-scattered plain is similar to the bird's African habitat. Males and females are almost identical and often take to the air together, but it is the flamboyant tumbling motion of the male's mating display that is most impressive. It flies vertically to a stalling halt, closes its wings, then plunges towards the earth only to loop again into a vertical position to repeat the dive. Females will not mate unless the male performs this display.

Numerous streams and waterfalls (left) are to be found in the mountainous region which contains the greatest diversity of wildlife found in Arabia, including the 11 endemic birds and many unique plant species.

The Sarawat Mountains rise to more than 4000 metres in south-western Arabia. Moisture-laden air from the Red Sea forms clouds which ascend into the juniper forests and clusters of tree euphorbia such as these in the Mahrit region of Yemen (left).

The small green frog, Hyla savignyi (above), is only found at high altitudes where there is permanent water, relatively low temperatures and good vegetation.

Leopards are distributed throughout Africa, Arabia and Asia in a confusing array of sub-species. The Arabian leopard (nimr) is one of seven recognized sub-species and, until recently, its range extended along the entire Sarawat and into the mountain areas of Oman (left). Shooting, poisoning and the walling up of lairs has taken a heavy toll in recent years and protection programmes currently implemented may be too late to save it from extinction.

Many Arabian reptiles like the agamid lizard (above) also have affinities with African species.

44

Above: Jebel Dibbagh, just south of the Gulf of Aqaba, is typical of dry northern Sarawat Mountains eroded by heat and wind. The exposed granite and the sandstone of the mountains is a principal source of sand for the central deserts.

The hamadryas baboon has a social structure second only to Man's in its complexity. An endangered species in Africa, there are more than 350 000 of them in the Asir region of Saudi Arabia where their range extends both for 500 miles along the mountain region and also out into the dry plains on both sides of the escarpment.

Lying as it does between Africa, Asia and Europe, Arabia has inherited wildlife from each of these regions. The Nubian ibex (above), a form of mountain goat, is of African origin and ideally adapted to the dry mountains. Renowned for their agility, they have cloven hooves which can expand to grip the rock, the soft inner pads clinging on like suction caps.

The rise and fall of surrounding seas periodically exposed and then covered land bridges between continents and so influenced migratory pathways. The Indian grey mongoose (right) may even have been able to make its way to the palm groves of Bahrain Island in the Arabian Gulf across such a bridge.

Euphorbias (above) are an Asian
form of cactus but are of separate
evolutionary development. Arabian
forms have both Asian and African
affinities. Some euphorbia types survive
today only on a single hillside or in an
inter-dependent association with a single
species of plant.

Overleaf: The African swallow-tail
butterfly flourishes in Arabia. Although
much insect life is shared with
surrounding regions, four out of ten insect
species found in Arabia are found only
there: a very high level of endemicity.

improve and the Sahara remained as a barrier. On the other hand, the migratory barrier of extreme aridity to the north of the horn of Africa was at this time countered by the creation of a land bridge, across the Hanish Sill, once more linking the two zoogeographic zones. A period of high rainfall and moderate temperatures which peaked around 6000 years ago brought increased rainfall to Arabia and North Africa in general, pushing back the desert boundaries. The effect was strongest however in West Africa and conditions along the Red Sea border of Africa did not improve sufficiently, however, to allow free entry of tropical African species via the Sinai peninsula.

For example, Arabia's butterflies have also been studied with a view to interpreting the peninsula's zoogeographic links. The conclusions of that work are very much in line with findings based on other animal groups. According to Torben Larsen, who has carried out extensive research into Arabia's butterflies, the Arabian butterfly fauna is 'predominantly Afro-tropical with almost two thirds of known species falling into this category'. This apparent bias towards Africa is entirely caused, however, by the large number of species living in the Asir and Yemen mountainous ranges of south-west Arabia. Few of these species are also found across the desert plains of Arabia's central region.

Not all of the butterflies of the south-western mountains are African in origin. Several have originated from the north, two of which are found only in Arabia. Among these are forms with relatives in the Mediterranean and North African region, as well as several bearing close affinities with Himalayan species. Of course, butterflies do cover great distances in their migrations, and it is not impossible that there remains some genetic exchange between remote and apparently isolated populations. The vast majority of Arabia's butterflies are either Afro-tropical or Palaearctic in origin, with only six Oriental species, all of which are strongly migratory. Several of Arabia's desert butterflies show remarkable adaptations to the harsh arid conditions prevailing in the region. Members of the genus *Apharitis,* for example are independent of green plants, their early stages living in ants' nests. Other desert butterflies have pupae which can survive in that phase for up to six years!

There are about 500 different bird species recorded from Arabia and each year at least 3000 million birds cross the Arabian peninsula on their annual migrations. Among these are many which simply use Arabia as a resting place on their journey, whilst others may spend a significant part of the year in Arabia, either breeding or over-wintering. Among the birds permanently resident in the peninsula are species which have distinct connections with other zoogeographic regions. The African grey hornbill, *Tockus nasutus,* is one of those species which confirms the biological links between south-west Arabia and tropical Africa. It lives among woodlands of the Asir mountainsides, at altitudes of up to 2450 metres, where it feeds on a variety of items including fruits, insects, tree frogs and chameleons. Of the 16 known species of *Tockus,* 14 are of African origin.

The Abyssinian roller (*Coracias abyssinicus*) ranges from West to East Africa, whereas in Arabia its range is restricted to the Tihama plain and mountain foothills. Those fortunate enough to watch this bird in flight may be treated to one of the most spectacular aerobatic displays of the avian world! Their courtship flight consists of a shallow dive from considerable elevation, incorporating a roll that looks almost like a somersault, accompanied by a raucous call. An equally impressive territorial display involves a stalling flight pattern; the bird plunging earthwards with closed wings before finally opening them again and recommencing a rolling flight routine. Rüppell's weaver *Ploceus galbula* is another African element also found up to 2650 metres in the Asir region of south-west Arabia and on the Tihama lowlands. Other African species include the white-browed coucal, dikkop, amethyst starling, red-eyed dove, and African silverbill.

Along the Gulf are found several Oriental species such as the Indian roller, white-cheeked bulbul and purple sunbird. The latter, *Nectarinia asiatica,* occurs in Oman, the United Arab Emirates, Iran and north-west India. The Palestinian sunbird (*Nectarinia osea*) is more widely distributed, from Syria in the north to southern Oman, with a separate race in Africa. The Nile valley sunbird (*Anthreptes metallicus*) is an Arabian resident which also migrates along the Red Sea and, as its common name suggests, also lives in North Africa, along the Nile valley. It is a short-billed species which often pricks the back of flowers to reach its food.

Among the most impressive of Arabia's birds was, of course, the Arabian ostrich, a species now sadly extinct. It too had clear affinities with Africa and in fact the African ostrich is being introduced to some areas in the hope of bringing back the ostrich species as a member of Arabia's wildlife. Whilst some birds have been driven to extinction in Arabia by Man, others have been introduced to the peninsula or have had their numbers greatly boosted by human activities. The Indian crow, for example, is now plentiful around some town and city areas, whilst the ringed parakeet is also on the increase in eastern and southern Arabia, perhaps as a result of escapes and subsequent wild breeding by caged birds.

Many representatives of African plants also occur in Arabia. The juniper forests of the southern Sarawat are similar to those of the Ethiopian highlands and the lowland vegetation of Yemen also has tropical African affinities. Indeed, the African baobab tree, famed for its water storage

50

capacity, is found both in Yemen and Dhofar. Perhaps the most important plant cultivated by the people of Arabia is *Coffea arabica*. To the locals it is known simply as *qahwah*; and to Europeans as coffee (a name possibly derived from the Arabic). Out of the hundred or so types of coffee only four are of commercial value and of these Arabic coffee is the most important. Despite the fact that its Latin name denotes an Arabic origin for the species, some botanists now consider that the plant first evolved in Ethiopia. According to this theory wild coffee plants were collected from Kefa (or Kaffa) in Ethiopia and taken to southern Arabia where they were placed under cultivation in the fifteenth century. An alternate story, now part of Arabian folklore, is that an Arab goatherder named Kaldi first discovered the plant when he noticed the strange antics of his flock. Around AD 850 Kaldi is reported to have sampled the berries of the evergreen bush on which his goats were feeding, experienced an exhilarating sensation, and duly reported his discovery to his colleagues. Up to the end of the seventeenth century almost all the world's coffee came from Yemen and, even today, despite widespread cultivation of the crop, Mocha coffee, named after the seaport from which it was exported, is the most prized coffee in the world.

As we have seen in this chapter, Arabia lies at the crossroads of three of the world's major zoogeographical regions (Afro-tropical, Palaearctic and Oriental) and is itself at the centre of the Eremic zone. The Eremic zone is the vast desert belt which extends from Morocco to western China. Arabia's present ecology reflects its ancient past, its current geography, and the influence of Man upon its natural habitats. The isolation of many Arabian forms in separate ecosystems has led to the evolution of distinctly new and exclusively Arabian species – the Arabian endemics, and it is these which provide the subject of our next chapter.

3

Adapting
to the
Land

Arabia's wildlife has originated from species which were already on the peninsula before it became separated from Africa and from species which have invaded the area since then. Cyclical climatic changes have altered the face of Arabia, both through rise and fall of sea-level, opening and closing land bridges with neighbouring regions, and through major shifts in rain-belts. These cycles of change have alternately allowed plant and animal species to range out across Arabia, and then caused a contraction of suitable habitats into isolated areas where environmental conditions remained suitable. Throughout this book I have used the terms 'Arabian species' and 'endemic species' to describe distinct life-forms which have evolved in response to Arabian conditions. The genetic make-up of a species can only be maintained in a reasonably homogenous form if there is continuous exchange of genetic material, through breeding, within the entire population. Once part of a population becomes isolated from others belonging to the same species, and the genetic flow within the species is broken, then, over time, the process of evolution leads to the development of new species.

For the past 12 000 years Arabia has been isolated from Africa and Iran by the Red Sea and Gulf, and from much of the north by extensive and formidable deserts of sand and stone. During this, and longer periods of isolation, many new Arabian species have evolved creating a unique aspect to the peninsula's ecology: that of endemism. This means that a remarkably high proportion of Arabian wildlife is found here and nowhere else, and it is these endemic species which have provided the focus for much of the conservation thrust presently taking place throughout the region. Once these species are lost from the wild they may be gone forever.

This almost happened to Arabia's most famous endemic species, the Arabian oryx. The largest of Arabia's cloven hoofed mammals, it is related to African forms. It lived around the edge of Arabia's true deserts for thousands of years, until, at the beginning of this century, the arrival of motor vehicles and rifles tipped the balance against its continued survival. During the 1950s large amounts of insecticide were used to control locust swarms in Arabia and this caused the death of many animals, particularly in Jordan. By the early 1960s it was quite apparent that it was only a matter of time before the last wild Arabian oryx was killed. Thus was born Operation Oryx, described more fully in chapter 12.

Arabia's gazelles seem to be in the process of developing into new species with sub-species already clearly established in some forms and others already recognized as distinct species. Thus, the Saudi gazelle is the peninsula form of the more widespread dorcas gazelle; and the Arabian sand gazelle is the local sub-species of the goitred gazelle. In both cases, as with many endemic Arabian mammals, the adults are slightly smaller than their related forms from outside Arabia. The Farasan Island gazelle is unusual in this regard, being very clearly an endemic species but also the largest Arabian gazelle. Another species only recognized as endemic as recently as 1985, is the Yemen mountain gazelle (*Gazella bilkis*), also known as the Queen of Sheba's gazelle. It too is a large gazelle, found only in the mountains of north Yemen.

Among the larger mammals, the goat-like Arabian tahr, *Hemitragus jayakari*, is an endemic species. It was first discovered in 1892 when Dr Jayakar, who was based in Oman with the British troops, purchased two hides and sent them to the British Museum. The living animal was not, however, sighted in the wild by European eyes until that redoubtable explorer Wilfred Thesiger travelled through the area in 1948. He identified their existing range as restricted to the mountains of Oman and on the isolated outcropping rocks of Jebel Hafit in the United Arab Emirates. There are only three existing species of tahr, one living in the Nepal Himalayas, one from India, and the Arabian species.

Arabian hares exhibit quite considerable variation in different regions and several sub-species are recognized which in time will no doubt evolve into distinct endemic species. The parent stock of all these forms is the Cape hare, *Lepus capensis*, and local sub-species include the Oman hare, *Lepus capensis omanensis*, which has large ears and a dull grey coat; and the sandy coloured Rub al-Khali desert hare, *L.c. cheesmani*.

The southern Arabian wolf (*Canis lupus arabs*) is also presently at the sub-species level, not sufficiently divergent from other wolves to be regarded as a completely separate species. It is nevertheless quite distinctive, being smaller than its northern cousin and showing some important behavioural differences. Unlike northern wolves the Arabian wolf does not live in large packs, but usually in pairs or small families. Inhabiting underground burrows, the female gives birth in the late winter or early spring, usually bearing four or five pups. They feed on carrion, small rodents, birds, reptiles, insects and even vegetable material.

Among Arabia's smaller mammals, Wagner's gerbil, *Gerbillus dasyurus*, is an indigenous species. It lives on rocky hills or mountain slopes and there appear to be one or two regional variations of the species.

As with the mammals, not all of Arabia's recent endemic birds have survived the impact of Man. The Arabian ostrich (*Struthio camelus syriacus*) – an Arabian endemic sub-species but a unique element of the Arabian faunal scene for thousands of years – is now sadly extinct. The range of the ostrich extended from the Rub al-Khali into the Syrian deserts. The ostrich played a significant role in the lives of the Bedouin who hunted the birds by traditional methods for their meat – an extremely valuable source of scarce protein for a desert people. In addition it provided an oil with medicinal properties, feathers which were sold to pilgrims, and eggs used as utensils. Rock paintings depict hunters in pursuit of these fast-running birds armed with a lance or stone sling: later a matchlock gun was used, but still there was a degree of equilibrium between the hunter and his prey. The demise of the Arabian ostrich, when it finally came, was rapid, unseemly, and extremely regrettable. The combination of modern rifles, modern transport, and a buoyant demand during the 1920s and 1930s for ostrich plumes effectively sealed the fate of this magnificent and unique bird, closing one chapter in the story of Arabia's natural history.

Other birds which are found only in Arabia have fared better and are concentrated in the south-west where there are eleven such species. They comprise a fascinating array of species. Three near-endemics include the Arabian warbler, Arabian golden sparrow and golden-winged grosbeak. Each of these three has populations on the African side of Red Sea. The Asir magpie is another contender but is only regarded as a sub-species despite the fact that its call is different from that of the European magpie. It also has less white on it, and its bill is broader. In addition, the Arabian accentor is sometimes listed as an endemic but may be merely a race of Radde's accentor.

Philby's rock partridge, a distinctly partridge shaped bird with a prominent black throat patch and pale to sandy grey colouring on its back and wings, lives only among the highlands of south-west Saudi Arabia and North Yemen. It seems to be an offshoot from the northern Chukar partridge which presumably migrated into Arabia during the Pleistocene period. The present high mountain population, mostly living above 2300 metres, became cut off from its northern relatives by the desiccation of

54

northern and central Arabian deserts. Over the course of time it evolved into a new species becoming one of Arabia's few endemic birds.

A related partridge, with a similar evolutionary history, is the Arabian red-legged partridge which is also the largest of the world's seven partridges. It not only inhabits the elevated ground of south-west Arabia, but is also found in isolated pockets in the mountains of Oman. Unlike Philby's rock partridge it can be found lower down the slopes, from around 250 metres, but also as high as 2800 metres where both birds may overlap. In general, however, the Arabian red-legged partridge tends to inhabit relatively fertile westerly facing mountain slopes whereas Philby's rock partridge prefers the rocky highland areas, primarily, but not exclusively, on the western side of the plateau. It is interesting that, despite their proximity to each other, the original isolated partridge population has already radiated to form these two endemic species.

The Arabian woodpecker is the only true woodpecker found on the peninsula, and is endemic to south-west Arabia. It is a well camouflaged, brown coloured bird, paler underneath, with folded wings displaying rows of distinctive white spots. Males have a red patch on the rear crown and back of the neck. It remains quite common in its preferred habitat, ancient acacia-dominated woodland, often in mountain wadis (valleys), or among cultivated areas of the western mountain sides. The woodpecker taps at trees to locate insects or grubs living in crevices on the bark or underneath it. The eggs of this species have still not been described.

The Yemen thrush looks, and indeed sounds, somewhat like a smaller version of a female blackbird. In the Asir it breeds among the juniper covered highlands and a few birds have also been seen in North Yemen, from 1200 metres to 2900 metres up, but mostly between 1800 and 2000 metres, always where there is plenty of tree cover. Its origins are somewhat confused, but it may be related to the olive thrush, which is distributed in a genetically linked series of semi-isolated populations across Africa. The Yemen thrush lives at the outer limit of this chain.

The Yemen warbler is an endemic species whose lineage is in some doubt. Indeed, it has only recently been confirmed that it is in fact a warbler and not a flycatcher! It occurs only in the highlands of North Yemen and the Asir mountains of Saudi Arabia where it lives among upland acacia and juniper. The bird has an unusual creeping movement, probing bark for food items, sometimes even hanging upside down like a tit. Only one nest of this shy, unobtrusive bird has ever been found and its eggs are unknown to science. Their survival is threatened at present by habitat destruction caused by clearing and firewood collection.

The Arabian waxbill lives along the lower slopes and up the wadis

55

(valleys) of the western escarpments in south-west Arabia, such as on the Tihama plain and slopes of the Asir range. Its closest relatives are all African species of waxbill and, like these related forms, it feeds on seeds of wild grasses, maize and riverine scrub. Frequently the birds cling to one grass shoot and reach across from it to feed on adjacent plants. They move around in flocks, often containing up to 200 birds.

The Arabian and Yemen serins are both endemic Arabian species, confined to the south-western corner of Arabia. Closest relatives are in East Africa and the Arabian serin was previously considered to be a race of the yellow-rumped seed-eater of East Africa. The Yemen serin lives among dry rocky country, often on open hillsides or around cliffs, where there is little vegetation. It also occurs around towns and villages, and has been recorded up to 3200 metres. The habitat of the Arabian serin differs from this since it clearly prefers cultivated highland areas. Both eat seeds, probably together with insects and some other invertebrate food. The Yemen serin has been observed to use old nests of the African rock martin, but very little is known about the breeding of the Arabian serin. Both species fly in small flocks, but there are usually more birds in those of the Yemen serin (which often accompanies the Yemen linnet).

The Yemen linnet is only found in south-west Arabia, in the Hijaz, Asir and Yemen mountains, and is common at high altitudes. Its closest relative is the linnet (from which it may be easily distinguished by the lack of red on forehead or chest) and it seems likely that the Yemen linnet is derived from an isolated population of the northern linnet which extended its range this far south during recent ice ages but was cut off from the parent northern stock by the drying out of central Arabia. It has a beautifully melodious song which is a delight to experience. Locally common, especially among the juniper woodland of south-west Saudi Arabia, the Yemen linnet frequently inhabits cultivated areas, particularly orchards and terraced wheatfields. Sadly, it is a species which is occasionally caught to be kept as a caged song-bird.

Whilst there are relatively few endemic birds in Arabia, other groups of fauna display a much higher degree of endemicity. Among the reptiles, there are at least 42 endemic species, with roughly 40 per cent of Arabia's lizards not found outside Arabia. The gecko genus *Stenodactylus*, for example, has four exclusively Arabian species, the Yemen gecko (*S. yemenensis*), the pale gecko (*S. pulcher*), the Khobar gecko (*S. Khobarensis*), and the Arabian gecko (*S. arabicus*). Two of the climbing geckos are also restricted to Arabia (*Hemidactylus homeolepis* and *H. lemurinus*). In addition there are two endemic Arabian chameleons (*C. calyptratus* and *C. calcarifer*). Five of the acanthodactyl lizards, which have spiny-scaled projections on their toes func-

56

tioning in the same way as snow shoes on the soft sand, are Arabian endemics. In all, 37 lizards have been identified as Arabian endemics. The majority of these live in the south-west of the peninsula, and are affiliated to African species. South-east Arabia (north Oman and the United Arab Emirates) has only seven endemic reptiles, all of which are lizards. Four of these endemics, and over half of the total number of reptile species in the Oman region, have their closest relatives in Iran. Of the 86 forms living in south-west Arabia, 36 are also found in Oman. Leaving these widespread species aside, 27 of the remaining 50 species are endemics. Reptilian colonization and evolution in southern Arabia has been primarily influenced by the opening and closing of land bridges across the Arabian Gulf and southern Red Sea during previous periods of sea-level fluctuation. Isolated by climatic changes, reptile populations adapted into exclusively Arabian forms.

As one might expect for creatures widely distributed by wind, Arabia's endemic butterflies are not quite as numerous in terms of their percentage of total fauna, as are the insects in general. By far the greatest percentage of endemicity coincides with the region of greatest variety of butterflies which, not surprisingly, is in the south-western corner of the peninsula, in the Asir and Yemen mountain regions. Of Yemen's 122 recorded butterflies, 12 are endemic species, representing 9.8 per cent of the total. In Arabia as a whole, 148 butterfly species have been found, of which 13 are endemics, representing 8.8 per cent of the total.

The subject of Arabian endemism brings us, for the first time in this account, to the marine environment and to the remarkably high numbers of unique species in the Red Sea and Gulf of Aden. The Red Sea, as we have seen in Chapter 1, began forming as a linear trough around 38 million years ago. The widening movement was at a rate of 1.3 centimetres per year per side. During the Miocene period, however, movement ceased and the Red Sea was still just a closed-off depression in which deposits formed from the evaporation of the sea-water. Around 5 million years ago the movement began again, at a rate of around 0.9 centimetres per year per side. At the beginning of the Pliocene era marine deposits were laid down, evidence of the Indian Ocean's incursion. Since then, at various times in its development, it was cut off again from surrounding seas and its level then dropped through evaporation, while its waters became saltier and saltier until few species could survive. The last time this happened was during the last glacial period, peaking around 18 000 years ago, at which time the level of the Red Sea was around 120 metres beneath its current level and its mean July sea temperature was a surprisingly low 3° Centigrade (surface temperatures in central Red Sea were probably around 13° Centigrade), compared with 29° Centigrade today! As global temperatures once more warmed, and the ice-caps began to melt again, sea-levels also rose and the Indian Ocean came flooding back in across the Hanish Sill, restoring marine conditions to the Red Sea.

Most of the Red Sea's present forms of marine life originate from this quite recent incursion of the Indian Ocean. The high levels of endemism reflect a very rapid rate of evolutionary development among the creatures which colonized this recreated marine habitat. For such speciation to occur, however, we must also assume that some form of geographic isolation also existed for the creatures which lived in the Red Sea.

There are many reasons why the Red Sea's life-forms have become, to some extent at least, biologically separate from those in the Indian Ocean. First of all the Red Sea is an extremely deep, long, narrow sea, with a bottle-neck entrance at Bab al Mandeb and a shallow sill north of there. Water exchange with the Indian Ocean is therefore somewhat restricted.

There is a paucity of nutrient levels in the Red Sea as one moves further north, together with the higher salinity of Red Sea water, compared with that of the Indian Ocean proper. The southern end of the Red Sea is characterized by sandy areas, green, nutrient-rich waters, prolific growths of seaweeds, but relatively little coral. The central and northern Red Sea is quite different from this, having clear, nutrient-poor waters, little algal growth, and plentiful corals. It is in these coral areas, isolated as they are from the rich coral areas of the Indian Ocean proper, that the greatest formation of new species has occurred.

Another interesting facet of this evolutionary process is that relatively few Red Sea corals are endemic in contrast to high endemism in other forms of marine life. In a recent paper on Red Sea corals, biologist Stephen Head lists only 15 species of reef-building corals which are likely to be endemics. This has been explained by suggesting that the present corals only returned to the Red Sea very recently, when temperatures once more approached their present level of around 20° Centigrade average (the lowest temperature at which reef-building corals normally live). This seems to have happened around 7000 years ago leaving little time for Red Sea corals to evolve into new species. Indeed, it is now quite clear that contemporary reefs in the Red Sea have built up only during the last 6000 to 7000 years.

Among the seaweeds, there are several unique types in the Red Sea. Along with coral, many species of seaweeds play a vital role in reef-building and provide food for many invertebrates and fish. Some of these have quite restricted distributions within the Red Sea region.

Among the molluscs, of which there are at least 950 to 1000 species living in the Red Sea, the rate of endemicity is around 5 per cent, rather low

58

compared to some other groups. This is explained by the fact that molluscan larvae, regularly washed into the Red Sea from the Indian Ocean, are constantly replenishing the gene pool in the Red Sea, and that the molluscan fauna is actually approaching a state of equilibrium with Indian Ocean forms.

If we look at some other Red Sea invertebrates, however – groups which are not in themselves so physiologically sensitive to lower sea temperatures as reef-building corals, nor with such resilient planktonic stages as many molluscs – then we find quite high levels of speciation and resultant endemism. Among echinoderms, for example, at least 20 genera include Red Sea endemic species. This includes 33 per cent of the feather-stars, 13 per cent of the sea-stars, 8 per cent of the brittle-stars, 2 per cent of the sea-urchins and 23 per cent of the sea-cucumbers found in the Red Sea. The average endemicity of Red Sea echinoderms is actually 14 per cent.

Red Sea fish have also suffered the effects of temperature and salinity changes during the Pleistocene era, with populations of those species which survived local conditions being effectively isolated from their counterparts in the Indian Ocean. There has probably been more time for their adaptation and distribution than for the reef-building corals, and there is a pro-portionately higher degree of endemism within their ranks. Seventeen per cent of Red Sea fish are found nowhere else (other than possibly the Gulf of Aden) and may therefore be regarded as endemic species. This reflects both the isolation which occurred during periods of low sea-levels in the Pleistocene, and also the unusual oceanographic conditions existing in the Red Sea today.

For the naturalist skin-diver, one of the satisfying things about the Red Sea's endemic fish is that it is often very easy to match them up with their Indian Ocean counterparts, clearly underlining the evolutionary processes which have created them. Sohal, the surgeonfish (*Acanthurus sohal*), a common and colourful species found in shallow water at the reef edge, is clearly the Red Sea form of the lined surgeonfish of the Indo-Pacific, *Acanthurus lineatus*. The Red Sea threadfin butterfly fish (*Chaetodon auriga*) on the other hand spreads through to the Indo-Pacific but appears to be undergoing gradual speciation, with many Red Sea forms lacking the prominent black spot on the posterior of the dorsal fin. The striped Red Sea butterflyfish (*Chaetodon fasciatus*) has already made the jump to new species status, being clearly different from its close Indo-Pacific ancestor (*Chaetodon lunula*). There are many other examples of such comparisons between Red Sea endemic fish and their Indian Ocean counterparts.

In this chapter we have been looking at Arabian endemic species and the causes underlying their development. In the next we shall be exploring a similar, and to some extent overlapping theme: relict communities which have developed in Arabia as a consequence of the drying out of the land and contraction of habitats in recent millennia.

———————————————

4

Islands

of

Isolation

There have been many cycles of climatic fluctuation in Arabia initiating an ongoing process of expansion and contraction of habitat and leading to the creation of both endemic and relict Arabian wildlife. As we have seen in the last chapter, by endemic I mean creatures that are found nowhere but Arabia and are thought to have evolved into their present form in response to Arabian conditions. The term 'relict' is used to describe those species with a range which may extend beyond Arabia but which have survived from a previous climatic age often in a geographically isolated and reduced Arabian habitat.

Relict species often develop into endemics if the pressures to adapt are sufficiently strong. Differences of climate and terrain, patterns of predation and different food sources all play a part. In Arabia, the evolution of endemic species has been further assisted by the contractions of habitat which caused mass migrations and isolated wildlife groups from the parent species. This process of change still continues today.

Significant climatic fluctuations have occurred over the past 100 000 years during which time, for example, estimated mean July temperatures of the deep Red Sea water have wavered between less than 5° and almost 20° Centigrade! Rainfall has also varied from periods of moderate precipitation to the present very low levels over much of Arabia. The current phase of hyper-aridity began around 17 000 years ago when the slow process of drying out the peninsula commenced in earnest. The trend was temporarily interrupted by a northwards displacement of the south-west monsoon, between 9000 and 6000 years ago, when even the Rub al-Khali enjoyed a degree of respite and a number of lakes formed in certain areas such as in the Wadi ad-Dawasir. From 6000 to 4000 years ago Arabia's climate became steadily drier and then the pace of change accelerated to such an extent that the peninsula experienced a period of hyper-aridity even more pronounced than it is suffering at present. Around 3000 years ago climatic conditions seem to have improved, since when cyclical changes have been less dramatic than previously and not exceeding a few hundred years in duration.

The physical geography of Arabia is itself extremely varied, ranging from deserts of sand or stone to high, forested mountain slopes and rocky peaks. The latter, mostly confined to southern Arabia, provide cooler, wetter conditions than those prevailing across the broad plains of Arabia, and there are isolated pockets of wildlife within such areas, survivors of eco-systems which extended across much greater tracts of Arabia in times past.

Examples of Arabia's previously extensive savannah grasslands are currently restricted to some upland, protected regions of northern Arabia and a few damp areas in, for example, depressions at the end of valley systems in southern regions. The once great forests which spread down into Arabia from the eastern Mediterranean are now seen only among the cool mountain heights of the Asir and Yemen mountains, or indeed the mountains of northern Arabia, in Jordan.

Extensive natural juniper forest, still surviving in the Asir mountain range, is a classic example of a relict Arabian community. It occurs throughout the westerly slopes of the Asir, above 1900 metres, particularly around Abha in Saudi Arabia, and is especially well developed around the summit of Jebel Sooda. On the upper escarpment, despite its location in one of the hottest regions of the world, temperatures regularly approach zero, creating frost during winter months. These cold conditions, effectively preventing the upward spread of many tropical and sub-tropical plants found lower down the mountains, recall the Palaearctic period. The vegetation which does exist has more affinities with Mediterranean and European plant communities than with the tropical zone. Whilst many such areas have been cleared for planting by local farmers, some of this ancient juniper forest still flourishes along the steep upper west facing slopes.

The juniper tree, *Juniper excelsa*, reaching over 15 metres in height, has branches hung with the lichen-like plant *Usnea articulata*, and leaves shading a dense undergrowth of lush grass and shrubs enriched by the exquisite Abyssinian wild rose (*Rosa abyssinica*) and the bright yellow-flowered daisy, *Euryops arabicus*. Scattered among the juniper are several acacia, olive (*Olea chrysophylla*), tree aloe (*Aloe sabaea*) and prickly pear. It is hard to believe, on visiting such verdant woodland, alive with butterflies and birdlife, that one is in an Arabia renowned for its harsh deserts.

As the boundaries of previously extensive forests retreated towards higher ground, woodland birds became isolated in their mountain refuges. Some, like Philby's rock partridge (*Alectoris philbyi*) evolved into distinct Arabian species while others like the Asir magpie (*Pica pica asirensis*) developed unique characteristics justifying their classification as local sub-species of more widely distributed forms. The Asir magpie is larger than European magpies, has a particularly heavy bill and a markedly different song.

Philby's rock partridge is a large handsome partridge, usually heard but not seen, living mainly among terraced fields on the east of Jebel Sooda on the Asir escarpment. It is particularly associated with fields of tall vegetation or stubble which are adjacent to rough ground and prefers more open terrain than its related form, the slightly larger Arabian red-legged partridge (*Alectoris melanocephala*). During summer one may be fortunate enough to catch sight of adult pairs of either species in flight over the juniper forests, escorting large families of young. The seven worldwide species of *Alectoris* partridge include these two Arabian species which are restricted to the relict Palaearctic communities of Arabia's mountains.

In a land where trees are at a premium one does not expect to find woodpeckers but the Arabian woodpecker (*Dendroocopus dorae*) is locally common among the surviving deciduous relict woodland of south-west Arabia which is dominated by acacia. They are mainly found along the western slopes of the Asir, sometimes in gardens or cultivated areas, nesting in several tree types, including fig. This endemic and relict species is the only woodpecker found in Arabia and, like the partridge, has evolved in woodland isolated by climatic change since the last ice age.

The Yemen thrush (*Turdus menachensis*) is related to the European song thrush, mistle thrush, redwing, fieldfare, blackbird and other members of the genus *Turdus*. Unlike some of these northern relatives it does not make major migrations but undertakes a vertical migration, moving to high ground in summer and occupying lower slopes in winter. An Arabian species, it is only found in the south-west, preferring areas of dense vegetation, breeding in summer on Jebel Sooda in Saudi Arabia, between 2500 and 3000 metres up, often nesting among junipers. It is clear that the species has evolved as a result of its northern ancestors being cut off, by the extension of arid lowlands, from the population breeding among the south-western mountains.

Yemen warblers (*Parisoma buryi*) are not as easily seen as the Yemen thrush since they tend to hide among the foliage of juniper and other deciduous bushes on mountain slopes, above 2450 metres. True to the best traditions of warbler behaviour, however, during the breeding season males take up prominent positions on high perches and their mellifluous song pierces the mountain air above the junipers. This is another endemic Arabian bird whose distribution is strictly limited to the south-western mountains (on Jebel Sooda in Saudi Arabia and in Yemen) forming part of the relict

Palaearctic community. The Arabian warbler (*Sylvia leucomelaena*) is much more widely distributed than the Yemen warbler and belongs to the same genus as the European garden warbler and the whitethroat. It tends to occur on the eastern side of the Asir escarpment, generally at around 2500 metres, among acacia woodland.

The Yemen linnet (*Carduelis yemenensis*) belongs to the same genus as the Eurasian linnet (*Carduelis cannabina*) and is common above 2400 metres in the Asir and Yemen mountains, particularly in cultivated areas. An endemic species, it is clearly closely related to the Eurasian form and has eggs with a similar pattern.

Another bird present at moderate heights (around 2500 metres) in the Asir, primarily among acacia woodland, is directly related to Arabia's ancient links with more temperate northern climes. It is the Asir magpie which has been taxonomically differentiated from its Eurasian counterpart (*Pica pica*) by its designation as a sub-species, *Pica pica asirensis*, causing some dissension among ornithologists who feel it is so similar to the northern magpie that it should not be taxonomically separated. As already mentioned, it does display slightly different behaviour, including a characteristic raucous call, and whether or not its status as a sub-species is correct, there is no doubt that it is a relict from the Würm glacial period.

Among reptiles there are several examples of surviving Palaearctic species in the Asir. For example, the dwarf snake (*Eirensis coronella fennelli*) is an endemic species living high in the mountains, above 2000 metres, from Al Baha to An Nimas. Neither it nor its original form, *Eirensis coronella*, occur elsewhere in southern or central Arabia. The closest records of the latter are on the Sinai peninsula and in parts of north-east Saudi Arabia.

A more dramatic example of discontinuous reptilian distribution is that of the skink, *Ablepharous pannonicus*, which is found in isolated areas of the Oman mountains and the high Asir but nowhere else in Arabia. Its closest other relative is from Basra in Iraq. Equally impressive is the presence in the Yemen highlands of the lacertid lizard, *Ophisops elegans*, which is found nowhere else in Yemen, or indeed in Saudi Arabia. Its closest other recording is at Petra in Jordan. It is confirmation of the ancient links between the mountains of south-west Arabia and northern wildlife.

The south-western mountains also harbour the remnants of some previously widespread mammals. The Arabian leopard (*Panthera pardus nimr*), an endemic sub-species of the better known African leopard and known locally as *nimr*, has been sighted, alive or dead, on quite a number of occasions in recent years in the Asir. Records range from that of a locally mounted specimen viewed in a pet-shop in the mountain town of Khamis Mushayt, to animals seen in the wild and reported by local people. The leopard is easily distinguished from the cheetah by a pale golden-brown ground colour patterned with black open rosettes and long tail with a black tip. There is little doubt that it was once more widely distributed in the western and southern highlands of Arabia than it is today. Apart from in the high Asir range, it is still present in North and South Yemen and in the mountains of Dhofar and Ras Musandam in Oman.

Questions concerning the origins of the Asir juniper community, and its present health have been nicely addressed in a recent study of local mosses and liverworts (bryophytes), of which there are 85 species in the Asir mountains. The bryophytes are indicators of vegetation conditions and the study of Arabia's forms, carried out by Wolfgang Frey, provides a fascinating insight into several aspects of the peninsula's plant life. Twelve lichens and seven mosses were found to be growing on junipers and on *Acacia origena*. Indeed, they form a prominent feature of the juniper trees, with bryophytes covering 86 per cent of their bark and lichens occupying 14 per cent! Most of the dominant bryophytes in this case are dry-loving mosses (such as *Hypnum vaucheri, Leucodon dracaenae, Leptodon smithii* and *Fabronia abyssinica*) and, interestingly enough, the situation is reversed on the acacia bark which has a conspicuous covering of lichens covering 76 per cent, with the bryophytes reduced in this case to 24 per cent.

Sociologically, the lichen-moss community living on juniper bark in the Asir has been most closely compared with a similar association in the Mediterranean region. It has also been shown from studies of European mosses that the 'pleurocarpus' forms covering this Arabian juniper bark are indicators of a natural state or one where disturbance has been minimal. Frey was pleased to report that the bryophyte and lichen community in the juniper areas were still in a natural or near natural state. The technique is now being used to assess the condition of other areas of Arabia's high woodland.

Along the wadi (valley) bottoms of the Asir's western escarpment there are remnants of a different period of Arabia's past, reflecting its ancient connections with Africa rather than the intermittent incursion of Palaearctic species over the past 80 000 or so years. Here a lush Afro-tropical environment is preserved in isolated patches of moist ground, dominated by large bushes of *Ziziphus spina-christa*, fig (*Ficus*), *Euphorbia*, aloes and others. In one such valley there is a small relict community of *Mimusops*, the only remaining specimens of the largest trees in Arabia, themselves indicators of the region's ancient links with Africa. And it is among these western slopes and valleys that the greatest concentrations of African birds are found, including the grey-headed kingfisher, bee-eaters, African grey hornbill, graceful warbler and sunbirds.

65

Today there are few permanent watercourses in Arabia, but the remnants of earlier lake and river dwellers still survive in refuges of isolated water sources. The peninsula's freshwater fish provide some of the most direct evidence of Arabia's ancient links with Africa and Asia since primary freshwater fish can only live in fresh water and must have been originally distributed along freshwater routes which have since dried up or been severed by marine incursions. Not surprisingly, in view of the long periods of isolation, virtually all Arabia's native freshwater fish are endemic species.

In the north, Azraq oasis in Jordan has about 5 square kilometres of perennial waterbodies, contrasting with the huge 4000 square kilometres lake which covered the region during the Pleistocene period. Today, water falling on the Asir and Yemen mountains drains through wadis to the coastal plain and Red Sea or eastwards, towards the desert where it sinks beneath the sands, flowing through underground watercourses. The Al-Hajar mountains of Oman similarly deposit their rainfall into the Gulf of Oman, the Arabian Sea or into the Rub al-Khali.

Distribution of primary freshwater fish within the peninsula has been used as the basis for recognizing three separate provinces, the Oman mountains; the Red Sea and Gulf of Aden drainage system; and thirdly the Rub al-Khali system. Each is characterized by a particular, albeit very restricted, assemblage of freshwater fish surviving as relict communities and reminders of a time when the peninsula was a much wetter place. There is little doubt that increasing aridity since the Pleistocene has eradicated many freshwater species and that those which remained found themselves isolated and subsequently evolved as endemic species.

As with fish, Arabia's amphibia, occurring in isolated freshwater bodies, provide firm indications of the ancient land bridge which the peninsula once provided between Asia and Africa. Six of Arabia's nine Anura amphibians are endemic to the peninsula with their closest relatives found either in Ethiopia or India. The two confirmed localities for the green toad, *Bufo viridis*, in Arabia coincide with the distributional range of other Palaearctic relict forms in the peninsula such as the magpie. It has been found for instance at an elevation of 3000 metres near Jebel Sooda, in verdant areas where juniper and acacia forests merge with copses of wild olive trees and where there are pools of perennial water. Along with two other amphibians, the Arabian water-frog, *Rana ridibunda*, and the tree-frog, *Hyla savignyi*, the green toad is clearly a survivor from the last ice age.

Relict Asian communities are predominantly found in eastern Arabia, around the oases of Hoffuf and Qatif, and on the island of Bahrain. The pond turtle (*Mauremys caspica*) is an Asiatic species found in ponds in Bahrain and at the mainland oases of Al Qatif and Al Hasa. Other relicts of the peninsula's ancient links with Asia sharing a similarly restricted distribution and dependent on proximity to water, are the Indian grey mongoose (*Herpestes edwardsi*), found on Bahrain and around Al Qatif, and the Asiatic jackal (*Canis aureus*) occurring near Al Qatif and Al Hasa. All of these were once more widespread but increasing aridity has shrunk their potential habitats until all that remains are these isolated communities, relicts of an earlier age. Several Arabian inhabitants of Asian origin have been lost during recent times: the Asiatic lion (*Panthera leo*) which existed as an Arabian sub-species, slightly smaller than its more widespread relative, disappeared from Arabia in the middle of the last century; the last Asiatic cheetah in Arabia (*Acinonyx jubatus venaticus*) was apparently killed in 1973.

In addition to climatic change, Man himself has created barriers for wildlife, driving many species to the margins of their previous habitats, restricting the range of species such as ibex to inaccessible rocky places, thus creating modern-day relicts. This is a theme we shall return to in later chapters.

Arabia's long period of gradual warming and drying out has caused ancient habitats to shrink and in many cases disappear. The peninsula is, however, so vast and has such a natural range of physical environments from high mountains to deep valleys and underground streams, that fragments of many previously dominant communities have survived in isolated pockets influenced by their own micro-climates, despite the major climatic changes which have occurred on the peninsula. Notwithstanding their restricted size and their isolation from their parent communities these relicts of an earlier age are of great importance since they act as reservoirs of biological diversity in which many animals and plants are preserved over thousands of years. Should climate take a turn for the better in Arabia, with temperatures falling and rainfall increasing, then many of these species will once more extend their ranges, re-establishing themselves as dominant forms in a newly enriched environment. It is partly for this reason that biologists place such great emphasis on the preservation of Arabia's relict communities of plants and animals.

5

The Great Deserts: Stone, Salt and Sand

Arabia lies at the centre of the largest desert system on earth, a vast region extending from Morocco to China. However, the deserts of Arabia are perhaps the most deprived of water for they are encircled by mountains which prevent moisture sources from crossing into the desert: in the west it is the high Sarawat escarpment, in the south the mountains of Yemen and Oman, to the east the Iranian Zagrab mountains and in the north the mountains of Turkey.

Within the Arabian desert system there is however an immense variety of deserts. Sand deserts occupy one third of the peninsula but there are also deserts of stone, barren volcanic wastelands, stony limestone deserts which are the most devoid of life and salt deserts which are the remains of ancient lakes and shallow seas.

All of these deserts are subject to extremes of temperature and have little moisture. Yet, despite these harsh conditions, life does exist there, albeit on a reduced scale, and the deserts contain many of nature's most highly adapted animals and plants.

The Rub al-Khali contains the world's largest continuous body of sand. Rub al-Khali means 'Empty Quarter' because for six months of the year, it is too hot for Man to survive its searing heat, shade temperatures rise above 50° Centigrade but on sand, grain temperatures which rise to nearly 80° Centigrade dare any living creature to move.

Even a modern traveller who stops his car and walks a little way can experience the space and emptiness and silence, the scentless wind, the stunning heat by day or the wonderful brilliance of the stars by night – the qualities which have influenced desert peoples ever since there were any and inspired the austere religions of the desert towns.

D. Howarth, 1971

68

At night there is rarely a cloud in the sky to retain the day's debilitating heat, the air cools rapidly and in the cooler months it can be freezing and the dry cold will painfully penetrate inadequate bedding.

Wilfred Thesiger travelled extensively in the Rub al-Khali between 1945 and 1950 in regions that had never before been seen by a European and in the prologue of his great classic of desert travel *Arabian Sands,* he introduced the Rub al-Khali with the following words:

> A cloud gathers, the rain falls, men live: the cloud disperses without rain, men and animals die. In the deserts of southern Arabia there is no rhythm of the seasons, no rise and fall of sap but empty wastes where only the changing temperature marks the passage of the year, it is a bitter desolated land which knows nothing of gentleness or ease. Yet men have lived there since earliest times. Passing generations have left fire-blackened stones of camping sites, a few faint tracks polished on the gravel plains. Elsewhere the winds wipe out their footprints. Men live there because it is the world into which they were born: the life they lead is the life their forefathers led before them: they accept hardship and privations: they know no other way. Lawrence wrote in *Seven Pillars of Wisdom* 'Bedouin ways were hard even for those brought up in them and for strangers terrible: a death in life. No man can live this life and emerge unchanged. He will carry however faint the imprint of the desert, the brand which marks the nomad: and he will have within him the yearning to return, weak or insistent according to his nature. For this cruel land can cast a spell which no temperate clime can match.'

The Rub al-Khali desert is approximately the size of France and its dunes are shaped by a variety of wind systems and sources of sand. Sand from the mountain regions of the Asir is washed by rare rainstorms down through wadis towards the desert where a single prevailing source of wind blowing in from the Indian Ocean has sculpted rolling ridges of sand which extend for hundreds of miles forming parallel corridors between which it is possible to travel with relative ease. In the central region the patterns of the dunes are more complex and less predictable but it is in the east that the most dramatic landscapes are to be found. Thousand-foot-high mountains of red sand rise from the flat, white salt-plains of ancient sea-beds.

Some plant species here are so well adapted that they can last for decades without rain. When it does rain, it must come at the right time as, regardless of the quantity of rain, most annual plants will not respond to late spring showers and germination is not triggered unless the whole season has an appropriate rain pattern. This is also true of many invertebrates like the triops desert shrimp and a multitude of desert insects.

The elusive beauty of the desert sand was eloquently described by Carruthers in 1909:

The colour of the sands, from a distance is pure carmine in the low morning light, changing under the midday glare to white and at dusk they appear wine red and of an intangibly velvety texture. But at close quarters the sands are every shade of yellow and red, blending softly into an amazing mixture for which one can find no name.

Within this hostile region, many of the desert animals have developed a capacity to live without drinking fresh water. Many, like the gazelle, can derive sufficient moisture from the leaves of desert plants, and also lick the morning dew from plant stems. In the most hostile periods of summer, both gazelle and oryx dig out and eat the newest roots of other plants.

The only people who have adequate knowledge to survive in the sands are the Bedouin of southern Arabia who live for part of the year on the desert's rim and in winter move into the centre in search of winter pasture for their camels. If rain falls at all, it does so quite randomly in the huge desert and areas of new growth are often far apart. The Bedouin locate areas where vegetation is to be found primarily through a social framework which involves the passing on of this vital information between the extended families of desert travellers. After rains renew the growth in an area, the plants which emerge from the apparently lifeless sand may provide pasture for up to three years. Today an increase in use of pumped water to create temporary pasturage for sheep grazing in the south-west of the Rub al-Khali has forced the Bedouin to take their milking camels further than ever towards the heart of the desert, in search of suitable natural grazing. One may be forgiven for asking how on earth the sheep get there in the first place. The answer is that they are ferried by trucks across the barren sands to remote sites where fossil water is pumped to the surface by modern diesel engines.

The Empty Quarter has always presented a major challenge to travellers of all kinds, both the Bedouin who regularly penetrate its edges but rarely venture to its centre, and to Europeans for whom it is a vast, unknown and totally forbidding desert. Charles Doughty, who travelled extensively in Arabia during the second half of the last century, eventually publishing an account of his travels in *Wanderings in Arabia*, commented: 'I never found any Arabian who had aught to tell, even by hearsay, of that dreadful country'. Its mystique easily captured the attention of that romantic figure, Lawrence of Arabia, who urged that one of the early airship flights to India should pass across the Empty Quarter: 'To go over the Empty Quarter will also be an enormous advertisement for them: it will mark an era in exploration. It will finish our knowledge of the earth. Nothing but an airship can do it, and I want it to be one of ours which gets the plum.'

70

Bertram Thomas made the crossing in the winter of 1930–31 and was soon followed by St John Philby who travelled in the opposite direction to Thomas, moving with camels from north to south. The airboats never made the journey and, as recently as the end of World War Two, no other Europeans had crossed the Rub al-Khali and neither had any aircraft flown across it. Wilfred Thesiger was the next Westerner to venture into this formidable desert in 1946–47 and again a year later.

Today the picture has changed but despite the availability of sophisticated navigational equipment and four-wheeled drive vehicles, only the Bedouin know the sands and remain virtually indispensable for crossing the Empty Quarter or any of Arabia's other sandy deserts. They have a vast knowledge of where it is safe to drive, and which sand areas are simply impassable, even to modern purpose-built desert-rovers. Crossing the Rub al-Khali today is quite a different experience from those suffered by the early European travellers, Thomas, Philby and Thesiger, who depended totally on camels or walking as their only means of transport. If one's camel died, it was virtually certain that the lone rider would also perish. Small wonder then that the Bedouin has developed such a close relationship and deep respect for these 'ships of the desert'.

Camels are adapted to desert life in more ways than are generally recognized. The notion that they store water in their hump is actually a myth. The hump is a fat store, accumulated when the feeding is good. While it is true that metabolized fat produces water, the process requires oxygen, and results in air saturated with water vapour being breathed out. In the dry desert climate water loss due to respiration accounts for more than the water produced by fat metabolism. The hump is thus more of a food store than a water reservoir. The concentration of fat in one place means that the rest of the body is not insulated and there is therefore a greater area through which heat may be lost.

71

The secret behind the camel's unique ability to survive in the desert lies in a combination of behavioural, anatomical and physiological adaptations. It is able to make the most of the sparse food resources of the desert, eating a wide variety of plants and grazing over a large region, rather than over-grazing in restricted areas. Camels will eat thorn bushes and dry vegetation which other mammals avoid, and can last for long periods without drinking water. This is important in creating a balance between desert vegetation and camels since it means that the camels are able to roam for considerable distances away from their freshwater wells, thus avoiding an over-concentration of grazing near the wells. In contrast, goats and sheep both contribute towards desertification. Goats, while being extremely hardy, are non-selective grazers destroying much of the desert's sparse vegetation, whilst sheep are selective grazers but are highly dependent upon fresh water, tending to bunch up around wells, causing over-grazing.

When a herd of thirsty camels arrives at a source of water they drink so much, and so fast, that one can see the water-level of a large drinking vessel plummet and even a modern water pump may not keep pace! Interestingly enough, individual camels are slightly slower drinkers than cattle, and a thirsty camel drinks somewhat more slowly than a well-watered animal. Measurements carried out on working camels in the desert indicate that a well-nourished camel drinks at a rate of 10 to 20 litres per minute and often takes in over 100 litres at a session. At temperatures of 30 to 35° Centigrade, camels can go for 10 to 15 days without drinking fresh water but as the temperature rises, the duration period between drinking sessions reduces. Of course, like other desert animals, they derive considerable water from vegetation and during winter months they may actually not drink at all, obtaining all their required water intake from food plants which may contain 50 to 60 per cent of their weight as water.

The camel's renowned capacity to drink large quantities of water is related, not to water storage *per se*, but to the need to replace water already lost. Rather than being able to store water for future use their physiology is adjusted so that water loss is minimized whilst tolerance to desiccation is extremely high. A camel may lose up to 40 per cent of its body water without perishing. If humans lose only 12 per cent, they die. A camel which has lost a quarter of its normal body water will suffer only a one tenth diminution in blood volume whereas Man under similar circumstances would proportionally suffer a loss three times as great causing human blood to become too thick to transmit body heat to the skin. Camel blood contains haemoglobin with a very high affinity for oxygen whilst the plasma is rich in dehydration-resistant albumin. When a dehydrated camel does drink large amounts of water, this is absorbed gradually into the blood and tissues which are able to tolerate a much greater level of dilution than most other mammals. The red blood cells are able to swell to 240 per cent of their initial size without breaking.

The major single source of water loss is through evaporation from sweat and respiration. Other sources of loss are through faeces and urine. It has been calculated that pack camels in extremely hot desert conditions lose 3.4 litres of water per day per 100 kilogrammes of body weight. The average camel living in midsummer Arabia, under what amounts to extreme heat stress, requires 20 to 30 litres of replenishment water per day. This is actually a very low rate of water loss and is achieved as a result of various adaptations. First of all, the camel's hair serves a dual role of protecting the skin from extreme heat, and dissipating body heat to the air. Sweat evaporates under the camel's fur, at the surface of the skin, thus maximizing the cooling effect on the animal's body. Temperature gradients measured across the fur can be as great as 30° Centigrade! A shorn camel actually loses 50 per cent more water per day than one still carrying its fur. Camels do not urinate often and they produce very dry faeces. Nostril cavities moisten dry air as it is breathed in and cool exhaled air, thus reducing water loss. In hot weather, body temperature rises during the day and falls again at night, thus helping to conserve water. Diurnal temperature fluctuations in dehydrated camels have been shown to range from as low as 34.2° Centigrade in the early morning to 40.7° Centigrade in the afternoon. Water loss through sweating is thus reduced, partially through toleration of stored body heat and partially through minimizing the difference between body temperature and external air temperature lowering the need for evaporative cooling. Desert gazelle and the Arabian oryx also display this diurnal variation in body temperature when dehydrated. The metabolic rate in camels is unexpectedly low: at least half that of a cow living in similar conditions. It is another factor which reduces water requirements.

The camel is the largest of Arabian animals. Whilst smaller desert mammals may hide from the full heat of the sun in daytime, confining their activities to the night, camels are too big to adopt such a strategy. Unless driven by Man however, their behaviour is geared towards water conservation. In hot weather, for example, they often prefer to rest throughout the day, thus avoiding exertion. When they do so they continually shift their position, throughout the day, so that they remain facing the sun as it tracks across the sky, exposing as little of their bodies as possible to direct heat. They may also lie close to each other since adjacent camel bodies are not as hot as the surrounding air.

The camel's anatomy is uniquely adapted to cope with the extreme temperatures which it encounters. Its long legs hold the body high above the ground and enable the camel to cover large distances with the expenditure of relatively little energy. At a slow gait camels cover about 8 kilometres per hour, whilst a medium pace is around 12 kph and a normal fast pace 16 to 20 kph.

Two other advantages of the camel's height are that it can extend its long neck up to the upper leaves on the highest branches of many bushes or trees, way out of reach of other grazers – even goats which mount trees with their forelegs. A camel's height also enables it to have a better view of the countryside, helping in the location of possible grazing sites. Its long neck is equipped with a peculiar arrangement of neck nerves and cerebral arteries regulating blood supply regardless of whether the head is lowered or raised. Large leg and neck veins are also equipped with non-return valves preventing, for example, blood in the jugular vein flooding the brain when the head is quickly lowered to the ground.

Among the camel's anatomical adaptations, there is perhaps nothing to rival the perfection of its most unusual eye. The eye itself is able to see at night almost as well as in daytime, its night-time vision being enhanced by the outer layer of the retina, whilst the blindingly intense light of the day is shielded from the pupil by a fringed iris. During a sandstorm, the eyelids are lowered to protect the eyes, but they remain translucent so that the camel can still see where it is going, even with its eyes shut! The eyes are kept moist, even in dry air, by a continuous flow of 'tears' from the lacrymal duct, preventing the eyes' surface from drying out. The ducts themselves are wider than in other mammals, reducing the likelihood of blockages from sand-grains.

Man's relationship with the camel began in Arabia around 4000 years ago. Their use as domestic animals is recorded in the Bible around 1800 BC, when Sarai, the wife of Abraham, is reported to have possessed 'asses and camels' (Genesis 12). The great difficulty faced by early navigators making a northerly passage up the Red Sea, battling for much of the way against prevailing head-winds, fostered the growth of camel-trains and the use of camels to transport goods which had been brought to southern Arabia by sea from Africa, India, or further afield. The incense trail was quickly established and the economic importance of the camel firmly entrenched.

It was in southern Arabia, isolated from the north by the vast deserts of the central region, that the relationship developed into one of almost total interdependence between nomadic Bedouin and their camels. They were used for transportation, battle, currency, wool, leather, milk, and for food. To the Arabs, the camel is truly a God-given gift, enabling them to survive in harsh surroundings. Indeed, much of the Arab success in the peninsula was directly linked to their efficient use of the camel. Even today, in parts of Arabia, camels retain an all-important role in the local economy. The Al Murrah of southern Arabia are an example of traditional camel herdsmen: people whose daily lives are dictated by the requirements of their camels, perpetuating a tradition of nomadism which has brought Man and the deserts of Arabia into such intimate contact with each other.

The traditional concept of deserts as being totally devoid of life is, as we have already seen, an erroneous one. During the making of the three-part film, *Arabia: Sand, Sea, Sky*, I was privileged to cross the Rub al-Khali on a reconnaissance survey, together with members of the Saudi Arabian National Commission for Wildlife Conservation and Development (NCWCD) and members of the Frontier Force. Our journey began at Sharawrah, close to the Saudi Arabian-Yemen border due south of Riyadh.

Equipped with three long-wheelbase Toyota Land Cruiser station wagons, a four-wheel-drive GMC Sierra Classic pick-up, a short-wheelbase Toyota Land Cruiser, a 10-ton Mercedes truck, three medium-wheelbase Toyota Land Cruiser pick-ups, a pick-up adapted for carrying fuel, and with Loren C navigation equipment, it was not in the style of earlier travellers.

Our Bedouin guide, Abu Saeed of the Beni Yam, had left his camel herd in the care of his son Saeed in order to accompany us. Abu Saeed's in-depth personal knowledge of the sands was to prove its value time and time again during the crossing. As we headed north into the Empty Quarter, driving at night across a gravel plain, our first dawn found us among a system of parallel dunes with a patchy winter covering of annual grasses and the drought-adapted resistant sedge, locally known as *andab* (*Cyperus conglomeratus*) and highly prized as camel fodder. It was nestling in the valleys, together with the spiky shrub *hadh* (*Cornulaca arabica*) and the saltbush *harm* (*Zygophyllum mandavillei*). Higher up on the slopes was the bushy herb *Dipterygium*. The long parallel corridors provided us with a convenient route which we followed, at times making good speed across a gravel floor. After six or seven hours driving the vegetation had become noticeably more sparse, and the previously dominant *hadh* had disappeared altogether. In this area we caught sight of a Rüppell's fox, some ravens and hoopoe larks, but apart from these there were few signs of life, principally signs of night activity, tracks left behind by black beetles, scorpions, spiders, skinks, geckos, houbara bustard and desert lark.

Our route continued to the north-east and by the following day the dunes had become less regular in their form, neatly distributed parallel formations giving way to a less ordered arrangement with more rolling transverse dunes greeting our view, making driving much more difficult. The dune system took its present shape thousands of years ago and it is only the surface patterns that change,

In a bleak, almost lifeless terrain, only a few *abal* (*Calligonum crinitum*) bushes provided relief. This leafless shrub, an endemic sub-species restricted to the Rub al-Khali, has shallow, well spread out, cable-like roots poised to collect water from the top 20 centimetres of earth as soon as rains have fallen and before the upper layer of sand has dried out.

Suddenly, towards afternoon, we re-entered an area of more prolific vegetation, once more dominated by *hadh*. Our guides commented that it has a particularly patchy distribution in the desert, perhaps due to the fact that its tiny fruit are not winged and are therefore less liable to be scattered over great distances. As we continued to journey north the sands darkened in colour and towards evening we traversed a well-known camel-grazing area known as *Hadh Faris*, where the vegetation was noticeably more prolific

75

and we even saw the prostrate herb *zahr* (*Tribulus arabicus*) sporting its conspicuous yellow flowers. This species flowers soon after rain and is greatly favoured as food for camels. It is believed by the Bedouin to impart a rich frothy texture to their milk. Most annual desert plants grow rapidly, flower, and seed within a month and die back quickly.

After two days of driving Abu Saeed brought us to the area where his camels were happily munching on the proceeds of a rainfall which had watered this section of desert three months previously. The ground here was scattered with *hadh*, green *andab* and flowering *zahr*. Already, there were many seedlings sprouting from the ground and the mature plants were in flower or fruiting. Watching Abu Saeed's camels browsing contentedly on needle sharp spiky plants, chewing at the tough desert vegetation, we were once again reminded of the animals' suitability for this harsh environment. Rather than completely devouring each plant, and in consequence damaging the desert's ecology, they took just a few bites from each, trimming them back a little, but leaving the basic plant intact so that its growth could continue. Abu Saeed was quick to explain to us the various characteristics of the different species upon which the camels grazed. Whilst *hadh* is a dry plant, lacking the succulence of other salt bushes, *andab* on the other hand is consumed more for its moisture content than for its food value whilst *zahr*, as already mentioned, is favoured for the quality it imparts to camel's milk.

In the very centre of the sand, at a well known as Umm Qurun, highly sulphurous water trickled from rocks to form a small pool – an apparent enigma in the midst of the world's driest desert, but offering little sustenance for man or beast. Despite the sulphur content, however, the resilient sedge *andab* sprouted from the pool itself whilst the succulent *harm* and leafless *abal* grew around it. Somehow or other both green sandpiper and Temminck's stint had located this isolated patch of acrid water. Also in the area we saw several toe-headed agamid lizards, temporarily anchored to the desert, body low, head moving slowly from side to side and eyes alert for the approach of dragonflies. After a period, the camouflaged lizards darted off a few metres to take up position at a new site. Hunting as they do out in the open, they are of course highly vulnerable to predation and must rely upon camouflage, together with a fast-burrowing ability, to avoid capture.

We remained for several days with the camel herd as Abu Saeed and his son gradually led them eastwards, towards Ghanim on the Oman border. This region of the Empty Quarter, described on maps as *Hadh Jimshan*, comprises low discontinuous sand-ridges running in a north-south direction, interposed on a pattern of rolling east-west oriented dunes. Plant life, in places relatively abundant, tended to cling to the northerly dune slopes and hollows and was once again dominated by the three main forms of *abal, zahr,* and *andab.*

Finally, after a few days with the herd, we broke away and entered the spectacular red-sand mountains of Mutaridah where towering 150-metre high dunes form predominantly east-west corridors across a *sabkha* and sandy desert plain. The *sabkha,* or salt flat, reminded us that all this region was once covered by the lakes lying between the dunes. As the water retreated during periods of colder global climates salt was deposited to form these vast, arid plains upon which sands later accumulated. Driving along the hard level *sabkhas* was reasonably easy but the occasional barriers to our progress formed by sand-banks proved to be formidable obstacles, particularly for the Mercedes truck, by now a universally regretted inclusion in our retinue! In the end, it became impossible to maintain our progress and the truck, together with a back-up vehicle, returned to Sharawrah, whilst we continued east, crossing the notorious Subqa Matti salt flats. Thesiger commented on the difficulties he encountered in this region:

> Here the salt flats were divided into three arms by crescent patterned drifts of sterile white sand. The flats themselves were covered with a crust of dirty salt which threw a glare into our faces and even, through half closed eyes, stabbed deep into my skull. The camels broke through this crust and floundered forward through black liquid mud.

In our case we sped as fast as we could over the thin crust of salt, praying that the vehicles would not break the surface and become bogged down.

During the four weeks in the desert we covered 3000 kilometres and saw no sign of rheem gazelle, oryx or of any large hoofed wildlife. Our Bedouin companions held the view that the rheem (*Gazella subgutturosa*) is now extremely rare in the Rub al-Khali, but is present in isolated pockets. Abu Saeed himself hunted rheem for food in his youth and told us how large herds of 150 or so rheem were once in evidence close to where we had begun our journey. The absence of oryx was of course no surprise to us since its recent rescue from certain extinction represented one of the largest conservation efforts ever mounted. One of the most perfectly adapted desert ungulates, the oryx has been successfully reintroduced in both Oman and Saudi Arabia. Whilst we have explored at some length the special adaptations of the camel, camels in the desert are nevertheless dependent upon Man to supply their water needs. The oryx, however, can survive for much greater periods without water. They take all their water from plants during the dry summer period.

Although larger mammals were nowhere to be seen in the desert, small mammals were still quite plentiful. Tracks or other evidence of Rüppell's fox were frequently observed together with several confirmed sightings of this magnificently adapted, silver-grey coated, desert predator whose large ears aid in dissipating heat, and whose hairy soles prevent its feet from sinking into soft sand. Rüppell's fox does not need to drink fresh water, obtaining its moisture requirements from plants and the animals it preys on. In addition to the fox, there were frequent sightings of the long-eared Cape hare (*Lepus capensis*), particularly in areas of vegetation at the foot of the dunes. The hare shelters among bushes but will dive into any available hole in order to escape predators. Abu Saeed hunts desert hares in traditional Bedouin fashion, using his saluki dogs to run them down. Cheesman's gerbils were also present wherever there was vegetation. Although they remained hidden in the daytime, their tracks gave them away and our identifications were confirmed when NCWCD scientists trapped several individuals. Like other desert mammals, gerbils are superbly adapted to a waterless existence. They can take sufficient moisture from desert plants, can consume dry food and conserve water by concentrating urine.

One of the striking features of life in the middle of a vast desert such as the Rub al-Khali is the echoing silence of the surrounding sands. It takes a little time to realize that the missing element is bird song. Few birds occur in the central desert and the most conspicuous was undoubtedly the brown-necked raven (*Corvus ruficollis*), a pair of which always seemed to find our campsites, announcing their presence with an occasional raucous 'craw'. Although they are quite widespread, they do require some form of tree or bush on which to perch. Hoopoe larks, so called because their barred wing pattern resembles a hoopoe's wing, were also in evidence throughout the desert. They are able to survive for prolonged periods without rainwater. What birds there are in the desert take water from the dew on plants and also feed on dune beetles after they in turn have fed on the morning dew. Had we been travelling this route 100 years ago we might also have seen the Arabian ostrich, at least along the fringe of the Rub al-Khali, but this population has probably been extinct since the middle of this century. Despite its large size, it was superbly adapted to desert life, obtaining most of its freshwater requirements from plants, and protein from lizards and insects. Another well-adapted desert bird which we did not observe, except for indications of its tracks in the south-western region, was the houbara bustard. Their numbers too have greatly diminished over the past few decades as a result of excessive hunting and disturbance of habitat.

Saudi Arabia's other two large deserts, the Great Nafud and Dahna, do not experience such extreme conditions as those of the Rub al-Khali and, as a result, support more wildlife. Birds like the cream-coloured courser,

78

stone-curlew and sandgrouse occur there. Their presence underlines the fact that water is not quite so scarce since the sandgrouse depends on reaching a source of fresh water daily. It prefers the safety of the desert to nest in however, and makes daily visits to a water source. Males transport water to their chicks by means of special breast feathers which function like a sponge. The presence and use of huge underground water reservoirs beneath the Nafud desert has led to its increasing development for growing wheat and other crops.

Whereas biological research into the ecology of the Rub al-Khali is in its infancy, presently pioneered by members of the Saudi Arabian NCWCD and scientists from ARAMCO, the Wahiba Sands are better understood, thanks to a series of intensive investigations under the general heading of the Oman Wahiba Sands Project 1985–87 undertaken by the Royal Geographic Society. The Wahiba Sands lie towards the eastern extremity of Arabia, close to the Arabian Sea on the eastern seaboard of Oman. It is a much smaller desert than the Rub al-Khali, stretching for only 195 kilometres in a north-south direction and 85 kilometres from east to west. A key difference between the Sands and the Rub al-Khali is that the Omani desert has more moisture due to the influence of coastal winds which drive moisture-laden air inland. Cold upward currents off the coast of Oman cool the moist air causing mists and heavy dew formation. In addition, the sands themselves have a very high calcium content derived from marine organisms. The result is a more diverse flora and fauna than in the Empty Quarter, with 30 species of plants recorded from the Wahiba Sands proper as well as 21 bird species.

79

Unique climatic characteristics in the Sands have nurtured a special ecosystem including several species found nowhere else on earth. Five beetles dwelling in this desert have been shown to extract their water requirements from the dew. Living on barren sand-dunes where there is apparently no means of obtaining water, the beetles construct little mounds and trenches during the night, perpendicular to the mist-laden wind and where dew collects. They are then active in the early morning, just before sunrise, taking in water before the day's heat once more dries up their sandy habitat. As the sun comes up the beetles retreat into the sand, 10 to 20 centimetres deep, avoiding the heat of the day.

The Sands form part of an ecological barrier helping to separate the wildlife of the western and eastern mountain systems. The Arabian tahr is only found in Oman but not to the west of the Sands. One of the most interesting features of the Sands are the isolated stands of a remarkable indigenous drought-resistant tree, *Prosopis cineraria*, known locally as *ghaf* and remarkable for its ability to maintain a rich foliage of green nutritious leaves throughout long periods of drought. Not surprisingly the tree has a very special place in the lives of people of the region who, when all other grazing has gone, may depend upon *ghaf* to provide food for their animals. *Prosopis* leaves comprise 14 to 18 per cent protein, plenty of moisture and are a good source of both calcium and potassium. The Bedouin often rest themselves and their animals under the tree canopy. These relict woodlands, surrounded by barren sands, are the only source of shelter and shade from the sun's glaring rays. In addition, their roots help to bind the dunes whilst *Prosopis* wood is used for building material and as fuel for cooking and heating.

Prosopis woodlands are a unique ecosystem within the Wahiba Sands, and the adjoining wadis, forming a major habitat for many of the other plants and animals found there. The extended canopy of leaves shading the ground enables many drought-resistant plants to survive throughout the year. Dew, forming in the canopy, drips down to irrigate the earth below whilst falling leaves, flowers, fruit and wood fertilize the soil. The trees also protect surrounding vegetation from the full force of wind or blown sand. When *Prosopis* flowers it is like a chequered flag to a whole host of insects and birds. The prime source of interest is the extremely nutritious nectar and pollen whilst the flowers themselves are mating sites for several insects including solitary bees. The tree produces large quantities of small toxic-containing seeds, a strategy aimed at ensuring that a few at least run the full gamut of seed-eaters to emerge unscathed and ready to germinate, although livestock seems to be immune to their poison.

The biological mystery at present is that there is a distinct absence of young trees among the woodlands. A possible cause is the intense grazing to which these areas are subjected. In this fragile ecosystem the introduction of domestic herds, trampling the soil and browsing upon young seedlings as soon as they emerge, has placed an unbearable burden upon the habitat. In order to prove that this is the main problem scientists fenced certain plots within *Prosopis* woodland. Less than a fortnight after heavy rain, seeds had germinated and twenty times as many seedlings survived than in the adjacent unfenced plots. But it is not quite this simple for within a month the *Prosopis* seedlings within the fenced areas had been smothered by faster growing herbaceous seedlings such as the prolific perennial *Zygophyllum qatarense*. Towards the edge of the shaded canopy however, the *Prosopis* seedlings showed more resilience, whilst the *Zygophyllum* was less dominant. A possible conclusion to be drawn here is that *Prosopis* woodlands were in better equilibrium when grazing was by wild animals such as oryx and gazelle.

Apart from the *Prosopis* communities, the Sands are colonized by a variety

Previous page, left and above: The Rub al-Khali desert is the largest continuous sand desert on earth covering an area roughly the size of France. In the eastern region the dunes rise more than 300 metres above the salt plain of ancient sea and lake beds. The dunes were formed by fierce monsoon rains during the last ice age. Surface patterns vary but the dunes themselves have altered little over the centuries.

The salt plains or sabkhas support little life but moisture attached to sand crystals becomes concentrated at the base of the dunes and can be reached by the long roots of desert plants (above).

84

Rub al-Khali is an Arabic term meaning 'empty quarter'. For six months of the year, it is too hot for Man to survive the searing heat of the sand. During the summer, shade temperatures rise above 50° Centigrade and sand grains can reach more than 80° Centigrade. In consequence most activity in the desert takes place at night and in the early morning when animal and insect life takes advantage of the desert dew.

It may not rain for 30 years in parts of
the Rub al-Khali but when it does the
water collects and is stored between the
dampened sand grains. It is calculated
that some plants are today drawing
moisture from rain that fell on the sands
more than 1000 years ago. This is
because once rain-water sinks below 2
metres, little further loss occurs due to
evaporation.

Above: Orobanchs *are a parasitic
family of desert plants which feed
entirely on the roots of other plant
species. Some are adapted to feed from
a single host plant type.* Right:
Calligonum *high up on the dune.*

88

Throughout much of the Rub al-Khali only six plant types are to be found. Most of them have extensive root systems and grow far apart from each other. In some plants, four-fifths of their mass is below the surface and roots extend to depths of 30 metres into the sand. The sedge plant (left) can withstand sandstorms which expose the upper roots. Other plants spread their roots across a wide, shallow area to take advantage of morning dew and occasional showers, dying back when the sand dries out. All minimize their surface areas to avoid evaporation and the Calligonum plant (above) conserves moisture with a white wax-like bark. However, heavy rain will not automatically stimulate growth and many plants demand an appropriate pattern of moisture throughout winter and spring before new growth develops.

Above and right: The tadpole shrimp is an ancient relative of the horseshoe crab and has changed little in the last 100 million years. Its eggs, which are no larger than a grain of sand, may lie dormant for 15 years or more. When rain comes the eggs hatch and within a few days they grow to adult shrimps nearly 7 centimetres long. Their life is desperately short as they must grow to maturity, breed and deposit their eggs in the brief life of a rapidly evaporating desert pool.

Many desert reptiles are most active at night and often have an ability to bury themselves in the sand during the day. Agamid lizards, like the toad-headed species shown above, belong to a large family of 300 species and are found throughout Arabia. Being cold-blooded, they tend to assume the temperature of their surroundings. In the early morning they warm themselves by exposing their bodies to the sun until the preferred temperature is reached. In pursuit of food they perch motionless waiting for prey. Attracted by movement, they dart suddenly forward to capture unsuspecting victims.

The population of many of Arabia's larger birds, like the griffon vulture, is falling significantly. Frequently shot by hunters, vultures, however, do not take live animals and have an important role in wilderness ecology. They feed on carrion and literally clean up the environment, reducing the breeding ground for flies and thus restricting the spread of disease. Often regarded as unpleasant scavengers their important role goes unnoticed.

The fennec fox (above) is found throughout the Sahara region but is extremely rare in Arabia and often confused with the young of the much more widespread Rüppell's fox. The fennec weighs only 1 kilogramme and is able to satisfy all of its water needs from a diet of insects, lizards and rodents. Like Rüppell's fox, it feeds on more vegetation than other carnivores.

The dromedary camel was first
domesticated in southern Arabia nearly
5000 years ago. It is superbly adapted
to desert conditions and feeds on a wide
variety of desert plants including the
thorny acacia (right). It can travel up
to 160 kilometres in a day. The broad
pads of the camel's feet spread its weight
and stop it sinking into the soft desert
sands (overleaf).

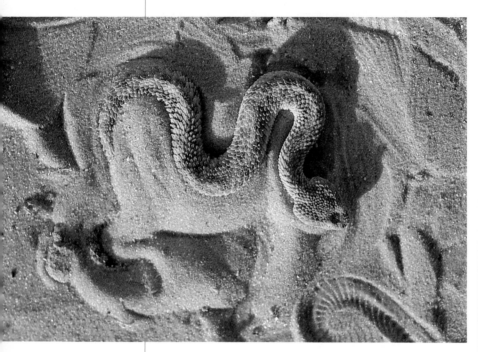

Few desert reptiles are better adapted
than the sidewinder viper (above). Its
sliding motion is a very efficient method
of passing over soft sand in which it can
bury itself while waiting for prey.

of shrubs and sedges, helping to bind the sands, and forming focal points for sand accumulation. Among the mobile dunes, there is a sequence of plant succession led by *Calligonum*, a species already mentioned as able to tap shallow water immediately following rainfall. On the leading edge of mobile dunes, where it is the first to sprout, *Calligonum* soon creates a mini-sandhill or *nabkha* around its base. As the mobile dune progressively advances northwards, powered by the coastal winds, it leaves behind an underlying layer in which the anchored *Calligonum* are effectively stranded. The more stable sands provide habitats for *Heliotropium* and *Euphorbia* which are able to survive so long as the sand is not too mobile. In areas of active sand movement these two species are soon smothered. Once they become established along the trailing edge of the dune, however, they compete with *Calligonum* for the ground's sparse supply of water. Eventually they win this battle for survival and the *Calligonum* bushes die back.

As previously indicated, the Wahiba Sands have a richer fauna than the desolate interior of the Rub al-Khali. Although deserts in general are undoubtedly hostile environments for most animals, those adapted to live there have the decided advantage of being able to do so without the intense competition which exists in more productive environments. This is shown by the remarkable success of the few species of carnivores living in the Wahiba Sands, particularly by the remarkable desert fox. The largest carnivore recorded during the course of the Wahiba Sands Project was the wolf, *Canis lupus*. By no means common and, sadly, hunted almost wherever it is found, the wolf is still just about hanging on around the perimeter of the Sands. Numbers are replenished from time to time by an influx of wolves from mountains north and east of the Sands but this is hardly a true desert mammal.

Since the Sands impinge upon the coastline, the marine environment contributes in a significant way to the available food resources for various desert dwellers. Red foxes, for example, are particularly abundant along the coastal margin and do much of their feeding along the rich marine fringe of the Arabian Sea rather than in the desert itself. Foxes were observed visiting the shore to dig up ghost crabs and molluscs, and to hunt for young turtles or their eggs. The red fox of Oman has adapted better than its northern cousins to desert life. Its small size, pale sandy colour, and even the growth of hairs between its pads, are more reminiscent of true desert foxes than this opportunistic species. Nevertheless, it remains concentrated around the perimeter of the Sands, leaving the interior to become the domain of the more highly adapted, smaller-bodied, larger-eared, Rüppell's fox.

During the course of the Wahiba Sands Project, ecologist Ian Linn

97

captured two male Rüppell's foxes and attached radio transmitters to them. The foxes, christened Walad and Shaibah, were inhabiting an area of the desert known as Dhabdhub where north-south oriented sand-dunes had a moderate cover of shrubs, each with its own surrounding mini-sandhill or *nabkha*. Among these were the tracks and burrows of various rodents, lizards, snakes, large beetles, scorpions and other arthropods indicating that there was a reasonable selection of wild food to support the foxes. (Later in the study, Ian also observed desert hares and even some gazelles.) Walad and Shaibah's vital statistics were recorded at the beginning of the study with Shaibah weighing in at 1.5 kilogrammes and a total length of 77 centimetres whilst the smaller Walad weighed 1.2 kilogrammes and was 75 centimetres long. The difference in size was later reflected in the behaviour of the two male foxes, operating in overlapping territories, with Shaibah clearly the dominant individual and Walad avoiding direct conflict with his larger competitor.

In addition to plotting signals from the radio transmitter collars, the foxes were observed during their night-time forays by use of special night-viewing binoculars. The foxes made their way from separate dens to a common feeding area at a brisk trot, often making detours to investigate a possible source of food. Where Shaibah spent long periods at the favoured feeding area, Walad only chanced brief incursions into it, always avoiding contact with Shaibah. From the radio recordings it appeared that the two foxes were aware of each other's presence at a distance of several hundred metres from each other. Shaibah apparently asserted his territorial rights in such a manner as to discourage Walad from challenging them, and Walad's strategy involved arriving at the favoured feeding zone earlier in the evening, before Shaibah normally appeared there. On one occasion Walad was observed making a very rapid departure from the zone, precipitated by Shaibah's unseen but later recorded approach. On another occasion during the study Walid's departure was quite leisurely and was followed several hours later by his return. This took place on the only night during the study when Shaibah failed to show up in the feeding zone.

Summarizing the results of this unique investigation of the elusive desert fox, Ian Linn commented: 'both these male foxes foraged alone, as would be expected where prey tended to be small, scarce and well dispersed ... Shaibah used a well-defined home range in a regular and highly predictable manner and had priority of access to the valuable food resource at the north end of his range, but was unable to defend it completely against occasional incursions by his neighbour, the slightly smaller male Walad.' Commenting upon the size of range of Rüppell's fox, Linn states: 'it is perhaps not surprising that a 1.5-kilogramme Rüppell's fox in the Sands needs a range as big as a European red fox four or five times its weight. Or, to put it another way, the food resources in 400 hectares or so of sand desert terrain can only support a very small fox, whilst in the cooler but much wetter climate of Europe a similar area can provide adequate resources for a fox several times larger.' If such a comparison seems to emphasize the paucity of resources in the Sands, it also makes this particular region look more like an oasis when compared with the stony deserts where a similar size Rüppell's fox requires a home range at least six times the size of that recorded during this study.

A mammal recently discovered in the Wahiba Sands, clinging to *Prosopis* woodlands, is the white-tailed mongoose, an African–Arabian species more characteristic of bush and semi-arid areas, but so far unknown in deserts. Its presence underlines the tremendous ecological significance of the isolated stands of *Prosopis*.

Carnivorous mammals and many birds inhabiting the desert depend to a great extent upon reptiles as a vital source of food. The Wahiba Sands Project recorded two toads and 26 reptiles, 18 of which were not previously known from the Sands. The toads came from irrigated areas at the edge of the Sands whilst the lizards and snakes were more characteristic of the desert proper. Sand geckos, such as *Stenodactylus doriae*, were observed hunting at night, often in strong winds and driving sand, painful to humans but apparently no problem for the lizards. In these conditions, sand-grains were regularly cleared from the lizard's eyes by a slow movement of the tip of its long tongue. On one particular occasion a horned viper (*Cerastes cerastes*) was concealed under a nearby bush, apparently ready to strike. A close encounter with an agamid lizard (*Phrynocephalus arabicus*), pursued for a few metres by biologists, culminated in it running behind a clump of *Heliotropium*, vibrating its body in a warning display and then sinking vertically into the sand leaving only head and neck visible. At a sudden movement, it disappeared altogether beneath the sand, vividly demonstrating the essential escape reaction on which such lizards must depend for their survival. Sometimes the desert sand is much too hot for comfort; however, the fringe-toed sand lizard (*Acanthodactylus schmidti*) can stand on sand too hot to touch. It lifts its hind toes off the ground, leaving only the heels in contact with the sand, and alternately raises its left and right front legs, giving them a rest from the boiling sand.

Five snakes were found in the Sands: the small, thin-bodied, pinkish blind snake, *Leptotyphlops macrorhynchus*; the harmless Jayakar's sand boa (*Eryx jayakari*) whose serpentine tracks are often seen on the soft sand; the sand snake (*Psammophis schokari*) with its fangs at the back of the jaw, making it unlikely to inject much venom into humans, and usually found in sand but also among trees and bushes; Gasperetti's sidewinder viper (*Cerastes cerastes gasperetti*) which eats small rodents and lizards and is itself vigorously pursued by the large monitor lizard *Varanus griseus*; and finally the viper, *Echis carinatus sochureckii*, seen here at the western side of its range.

Whilst both the Rub al-Khali and the Wahiba Sands are essentially low-lying, the Tuwaiq escarpment, in the centre of Arabia, extending north and south of Riyadh, is a raised desert with a limestone escarpment. Its prominent cliff-faces, sometimes as high as 150 metres or more, remind one of America's Grand Canyon. Among the dry, arid rock-strewn plain towards the south of the escarpment, known as Al Arid, a different type of desert fauna is found, including birds such as sand partridge, desert larks and the white-crowned black wheatear. Further north, towards a slightly wetter region of the escarpment, fan-tailed ravens and house buntings, birds one does not normally associate with a desert environment, are in abundance. The stony cliffs provide attractive nesting sites for other birds such as Hume's tawny owl, the long-legged buzzard and the barbary falcon. Winter rains, more dependable here than in the lower deserts, may form wadis and sometimes even permanent pools such as the lake at Karrarah.

The most forbidding of all deserts, with the exception of parts of the Rub al-Khali, are the lava fields or *harrats*: extensive lava, basalt and gravel plains pockmarked by volcanic hills and extinct volcanoes, sterile *sabkhas* occupying their valleys and craters. Exposed to the weather, *harrats* are cold and windswept in winter and intolerably hot in summer. Yet in the spring after rain falls, there is an explosion of life, with wild flowers filling the cracks between rocks, and for a few weeks the *harrats* provide a temporary refuge and breeding site for many nomadic birds. Harrat al Harrah in northern Saudi Arabia is a classic example and a 17000 square kilometre area is now under the protection of the NCWCD as a special nature reserve. The motivating force behind its protection was its importance as a typical laval plain eco-system. It was also one of the last places where the Arabian ostrich survived in the wild, prior to its local extinction around 1939. The recent ban on goat or sheep grazing within the vast *harrat* has heralded an impressive revival of its natural vegetation and animal life. It is hoped that the recent improvement in ground cover will also encourage more successful breeding of houbara since this is one of the few areas left in Arabia with natural breeding populations of this bird.

Eight species of desert larks also breed there, the highest number for any of Arabia's varied ecosystems, and making it one of the most important regions for larks in the entire northern hemisphere. Most of the larks nest on the ground, among the black basalt rocks, so the absence of trees does not create a problem for them. Common breeders include Dunn's Lark, the bar-tailed lark, Temminck's horned lark, the bimaculated lark, the thick-billed lark and the lesser short-toed lark. It is not really clear quite why the larks are so successful in this environment but their presence, together with that of several small mammals, remains an encouragement for some impressive predators including the golden eagle, kestrel, long-legged buzzard, litttle owl and the eagle owl. A considerable population of both wolves and foxes also inhabits the *harrat*.

In this chapter we have taken a brief look at some of Arabia's deserts, areas where one expects to find little life, but in fact discovers a whole host of species adapted to survive the harsh conditions and successfully overcoming the physiological constraints caused by severe heat and lack of fresh water. In the next chapter we shall be looking at a totally different habitat within Arabia, places where snow falls have occurred, and where conditions are far more favourable for the nourishment of wildlife, Arabia's mountainous regions.

6

The
Mountain
Barriers

The high mountains of the Sarawat and Oman act both as cloud traps extracting moisture from rising air and as a barrier preventing rain from reaching much of the interior of the peninsula. Thus, whilst their ecologies differ markedly from those of the deserts, there is in fact a close relationship between the two for the mountains are responsible in many ways for the creation of Arabia's extensive deserts.

The longest mountain system in Arabia is the Sarawat, a ridge of high ground extending for 2000 kilometres along the western boundaries of the peninsula. This escarpment, formed by uplift of the Arabian shield, has precipitous westerly slopes, in places forming 500-metre high cliffs, and a gradually sloping eastern edge. Standing in the cool depths of a juniper forest, surrounded by dense greenery and mellifluous bird song, it is a varied proof of the great diversity of ecosystems in Arabia. The towering juniper trees of the southern Sarawat seem permanent enough and yet these magnificent woodlands are in fact mere remnants of a previously extensive forest terrain which flourished thousands of years ago when the climate was both cooler and wetter. As annual rainfall diminished the forests, which once cloaked lower ground, died back until all that remained was the higher relict woodland restricted to the uppermost reaches of these moisture-laden mountains.

The impressive juniper forests not only contracted due to natural climatic change but they were also cut down by Man, partially for firewood or building materials, but primarily to clear land for cultivation. Drawn to this unique zone of cool air and fertile soil, an expanding population was forced to maximize the agricultural potential of the high mountains and it was the ancient juniper forests which suffered. Today the junipers flourish primarily on the steepest and most inaccessible slopes, untamable by even the most determined of local farmers. The Asir mountains, which link south-west Saudi Arabia and Yemen, are the only mountain range in the whole of Arabia to support such a dense growth of juniper trees and reflect the unique climatic conditions. Despite their location in one of the driest regions of the world, the mountains trap water from three separate moisture systems: evaporation from the Red Sea, climatic effects of the Mediterranean depression; and from the south-west monsoons which bring up moisture-laden air from the Indian Ocean. The combined influence of all this moisture over the mountains is an annual rainfall in the Asir of 300 to 500 millimetres compared to an average of only 100 millimetres in the central region.

While filming by helicopter along the crest of the escarpment, we were struck by a great contrast between the richly forested and cultivated western escarpment and the barren plains on the eastern side, emphasizing the rain-barrier effect of the ridge. The forest is at its most prolific along the top of the Asir range, at around 3000 metres, particularly where clouds are funnelled into pockets in the cliff face, but also on south-facing shaded slopes such as along the Raidah escarpment. A prominent feature of the highest forest canopy is that it is almost universally draped with the lichen-like plant *Usnea articulata*. Some of the junipers grow to 15 metres tall and they form effective dew traps, capturing water from the clouds which then drips down to the ground below, creating a rich undergrowth including wild roses and flowering shrubs. Mixed with the juniper are some acacia trees and olive and fig lower down. In these high altitudes where winter frosts are by no means uncommon, few tropical plants penetrate and most of the flora has Mediterranean and Eurasian affinities despite the fact that it has remained cut off from these more northerly ecosystems for at least 10 000 years. This isolation has resulted in the evolution of new and endemic species of plants and animals. The scientific importance of the southern Asir has been recognized and it now forms the heart of the Asir National Park.

As we have observed in the chapter on Arabian endemism, this area of remnant woodland has the highest level of endemism among all Arabian wildlife groupings. The Asir magpie, similar to a European magpie except for its call, lives in the highest part of the juniper forest. Golden-winged grosbeak, Yemen thrush and Yemen linnet all breed here. Also present are the red-legged partridge, olive pigeon, dusky turtle dove, little rock thrush, Yemen warbler, brown and woodland warblers. Both the olive pigeon and the golden-winged grosbeak feed on juniper berries.

Despite the best efforts of conservation authorities, all is not well in the juniper forest. The crowns of some of the older trees are dying back, perhaps indicating that the desiccation process which has been taking place for the past few thousand years in Arabia still continues. Improved accessibility to the forests, resulting from Saudi Arabia's gigantic road building programme, has brought new disturbances for wildlife in the form of new agriculture, cutting of trees and the presence of road traffic and increasing numbers of sheep and goats.

One possible indication of environmental changes taking place in the Asir is the recent reduction in the numbers of large birds of prey, such as griffon and Egyptian vultures. They were frequently observed here as recently as ten or fifteen years ago but now they are considerably less common. Even the large lammergeyer vulture, also known as the bone-breaker bird, due to its habit of picking up bones of carrion and dropping them from a great height in order to crack them open to expose the rich marrow, used to be present here but has not been reported for several years. Its decline within the region has been assiduously recorded by ornithologist Michael Jennings, chief coordinator of the *Atlas of Breeding Birds of Arabia*. He first noticed a reduction in lammergeyer numbers around 1980 and believes that disturbance of their habitat, possibly related to road construction and easy access to the high escarpment within the national park, may have caused large breeding birds to relocate. These large and highly specialized raptors seem to have been displaced by more adaptable birds of prey such as the ubiquitous black kite and indeed the fan-tailed raven, both of which are quite happy to live in close association with Man. These two are the most conspicuous birds along the escarpment edge, but other raptors can still be seen, riding the thermal air currents, rising up over the Tihama plain.

One form of wildlife which has prospered as a result of Man's increased presence among the mountains of south-west Saudi Arabia is the hamadryas baboon. Indeed, their numbers have increased whilst those of other large mammals, including their predators, have diminished. The baboons sleep in caves along rocky ledges of the escarpment and are sometimes even found sleeping in fig trees. This is possibly because of the absence of predators. They emerge at first light to greet the dawn with their chattering calls. It was this aspect of their behaviour, heralding the first light of day, which caused the ancient Egyptians to regard them as sacred animals. Whereas the hamadryas baboon is a threatened species in the other part of its range, in Ethiopia, in sections of its localized Arabian habitat it is regarded as a pest. Whilst they live primarily in the mountains, they also descend from there to raid the farms and wild fig trees lower down the slopes, towards the Tihama plain in the west; eastwards over the back slopes of the escarpment to areas bordering the central desert; and even northwards to the southern Hijaz mountains.

The social life of hamadryas baboons has been studied in detail by biologists working with the Saudi Arabian NCWCD, leading to some interesting results. Unlike other species of African baboons the hamadryas females are monogamous, remaining faithful to a single male in an exclusive and permanent relationship. The males on the other hand, as with all other baboons, gather females into a family unit comprising the single adult male, several females and their young. Young immature males show the first signs of forming their own groups by setting about kidnapping baby baboons from established family units. They groom and care for these just as long as they are able to hang on to them. Whereas younger males kidnap male babies, older, sub-adult males capture female juveniles and as these grow up they become the basis for new family groups. When mature, it is these females which groom the male partner. In the early morning, after the baboons have warmed themselves in the first rays of direct sunlight, the troop disperses to feed with bands of 40 to 100 or more animals moving off together through the trees.

This social existence has developed in relation to the basic requirements of sleeping, eating, breeding and escaping predation. Their erstwhile predators, the Arabian leopard and striped hyena, are, however, quite rare in the mountains today. Numbers are controlled by disease, accidents and lack of water in the drier areas. Increased cultivation and animal husbandry among the local population has encouraged active hunting of these animals as well as disturbing their wild habitat. Sadly, much of this hunting has been misguided since the striped hyena lives primarily upon carrion, vegetable matter and a range of small animals such as insects and reptiles, probably only resorting to killing large mammals when it is starving. The Arabian leopard, recently observed in the central Sarawat, and still surviving in the Yemen and Omani mountains, eats hyrax, hares, rodents, reptiles and birds. It is sad to report that the Arabian leopard has been consistently hunted by poisoning, snaring and by walling up sleeping lairs. The baboon's highly social behaviour, in which males group together for defensive purposes, seems to be relatively effective against leopards which will generally only attack stray members of a group.

The absence of predators is a possible reason why the hamadryas baboon in Arabia does not have such inaccessible sleeping lairs as its Ethiopian cousins. Indeed, many of Saudi Arabia's baboons have become perfectly accustomed to the presence of Man, even depending upon him for food: gathering at town rubbish dumps, or waylaying cars on the main mountain roads, begging for free hand-outs. Their appearance and behaviour endear them to many day-trippers who perhaps do not realize that the baboons can be aggressive defenders of their young and have been known to attack people who mistakenly believed them to be entirely harmless.

In remote mountainous regions the baboons are more wary of humans. If approached too closely, dominant males armed with fearsome canine teeth will lunge at intruders and, if pressed, the males will gather together to defend their patch. Similar behaviour is displayed within the species, fights often breaking out in pursuit of a particular female and on occasion a subordinate male thus capturing a dominant male's harem. Clans are formed by loose affiliation of several family units and the males within the clan will then join forces to prevent any other male from capturing members of their harems. Not all the fighting is confined to males however since females will fight each other, both for food and for their mate. Much of the baboon's day is taken up with less agitated behaviour, often with females carefully grooming males or with males signalling their friendship to other males or females. Young baboons spend a great deal of time playing and their games provide training for the social skills needed in later life.

The natural charm of the Asir, a region of Arabia which has been visited by relatively few Westerners, was nicely encapsulated in a letter written to a friend by British ornithologist, Arthur Stagg, who has been a prominent member of the Riyadh-based Desert Ramblers for several years, and who has made a significant contribution to our knowledge of Arabian birdlife. I am grateful to him for permission to quote from this personal account of a journey from Abha, across the top of the Sarawat escarpment, and down its western face, into the wadi (dry river valley) and across the coastal plain to the shores of the Red Sea. Such weekend nature watching trips have become increasingly popular among many expatriates, living and working in the Kingdom. This particular journey took place several years ago, before the recent disappearance of raptors such as the lammergeyer.

Commencing from Abha, the capital of the Asir Province, which sits at an altitude of some 7000 feet, we start the ascent of Mt Soodah. This in itself is an unspectacular eminence with a winding road to its peak and onwards down to meet the Taif road. However, it is an area of great charm. The wayside fields have been diligently terraced over countless centuries and wild flowers grow in profusion everywhere; gnarled and twisted junipers dot the slopes and from these occasionally burst, on noisy wings, a dusky turtle dove put to flight by a shepherd's sling shot or perhaps a prowling raptor. The clinging aroma of spicy-scented *Hypericum* hangs in the air and around their yellow flowers dart iridescent blue, orange-tufted sunbirds, calling all the while with an urgent 'jizz-jizz-jizz'. The call of Philby's chukar, the laughing chant of the palm dove and the starling-like whistles and rasps of Rüppell's weaver mix and mingle with the bleat of sheep and the incessant hum of innumerable insects. As we follow the road, mourning wheatear duck from sight and a hoopoe raises his crest in momentary concern. It is hard to believe that this is Saudi Arabia.

The road winds steadily upwards past stone watchtowers and gaily painted dwellings, past brightly dressed shepherdesses, their heads crowned with broad-brimmed straw hats to shield them from the virtually unfiltered rays of the sun. The juniper thickens and here it is that the gold-winged grosbeak breeds cheek by jowl with the Yemen thrush and the Yemen linnet.

We are now at 10000 feet and the road takes us close to the edge of the escarpment. The trill of black kite and the calls of fan-tailed and brown-necked ravens echo along the ridge as they ride air currents sweeping up from the wadi 5000 feet below. There, like a brown ribbon, the track winds and twists its way along the wadi bed, marking the route we shall follow. As we gaze upon the scene first one and then another griffon vulture rushes past at eye level and with a woosh of air: a bird so ugly on the ground, but oh so majestic in flight. On some days a lammergeyer haunts this ridge, truly the king of all vultures.

The descent to the wadi below is a hard, jolting ride around seemingly never-ending bends. There is little time for birdwatching but occasionally the orange patched wings of Tristram's grackle flash against the jebel and catch the eye, or the musical call of a blackstart reaches the ear.

At the bottom of the escarpment the temperature is 10°F or so higher and the air feels considerably moister. It is time for a drink and what better place than under the broad spread of an ancient fig tree. This one has fruit in every stage of growth and close scrutiny reveals a quite remarkable selection of birds feeding in the canopy. Colourful Bruce's green pigeon and Arabian woodpecker gorge on the ripe fruit; white-throated bee-eater take their toll of insect life attracted by the fresh blossom and over-ripe figs; bulbul and a host of assorted warblers flit among the leaves; here a handsome male amethyst starling with his much more sombrely dressed mate beside him; there a barred flank surmounted by green catches the eye – it is a none too common klaas cuckoo.

I could stay here for hours and frequently do. But today we must press on. Now and then stopping to check on a bird or butterfly, or to photograph a scene, or to chat with the locals, we steadily edge towards the sea. As we descend lower and lower, lush vegetation and fields of millet give way to acacia and camel thorn. This somewhat drabber scene is brightened by colourful shining- and Nile valley-sunbirds and the wadi resounds to the strange calls of the grey hornbill.

We arrive at our next refreshment point. Here a spring wells from the ground and as we approach a troop of baboon move away from the water barking in annoyance. A shaggy old male stands and glowers at us as the females, many with young on their backs, move off through the scrub. An amorous donkey makes a pass at a grazing female and receives a double

107

hoofer for his troubles. A trailing ribbon rushes from an acacia and back again, or so it seems. It is in fact a very handsome cock paradise flycatcher. Following its flight my eye alights on a small grey bird huddled close to the trunk of a tree. It is a gabar goshawk, doubtless waiting to feast upon some unsuspecting weaver.

We leave the waterhole and press on across a dusty plain. Here, on my last trip, I saw my first pied crested cuckoo and renewed acquaintance with the bateleur eagle. This time it's a pair of Lichtenstein's sandgrouse which provides an addition to my Saudi list.

Ahead lies Mahayle. We skirt the town and pick a wadi a few kilometres on. Here it runs with water all the year around and although some 50 kilometres from the sea is frequented for much of the time by pink-backed and white-pelicans, by egret, spoonbill and hammerkop.

We make camp well away from civilization, close by a dead fig tree washed downstream by some past great flood. It provides aromatic kindling which under the stars gives a friendly light and serves to deter insects and other creatures. It also proves to be the favourite perch of a grey-headed kingfisher who announces his presence at first light with an explosive trill. He is shortly joined by a pair of little green bee-eater which make frequent sallies in pursuit of numerous insects. A musical chatter reveals a huddle of silverbills, fresh from bathing in the stream, close-packed along a branch like beads on a string. The shuffling movements in a nearby creeper swims into focus in the glasses and proves to be a coucal.

We break camp and move off. Now we are back on an asphalt road moving towards the sea through a different type of terrain. Beehive huts, which reveal the locals' early origins, sit in close-knit clusters, some incongruously supporting television aerials. Around them black kite and Egyptian vulture circle in endless anticipation; a flash of blue draws the eye to an Abyssinian roller.

We pull into a sandspit which overlooks both the sea and a landlocked lagoon. The palms give us shelter and we make a brew. Over the lagoon five greater flamingo wade, busily feeding, bills reversed on the sandy bed. Pelicans sit dozily in the sun whilst on the fringe of the lagoon, kentish and ringed plover run fussily to and fro.

On the shore handsome black and white crabplovers stand in the shallows. On the coral reef herons sit huddled, dwarfed by a goliath heron which stands gazing intently into the water. Overhead swift and caspian tern scold while out in the deeper water a straggling line of brown boobies dive repeatedly on a passing shoal of fish.

Arthur Stagg's perceptive account of a weekend sortie from his home-base in the mountains at Abha to the Red Sea vividly illustrates the great wealth of wildlife and beauty which exists in this south-west corner of Saudi Arabia.

Moving east away from the escarpment crest in the opposite direction to the Red Sea, one is greeted by an entirely different picture. A few hundred metres from where the mist burns off, juniper disappears. These more gentle slopes are terraced and cultivated all along the upper reaches of the escarpment. In those areas which have been left wild, acacias grow, providing good cover for Arabian woodpeckers, blackstarts, Arabian warblers, flycatchers and the Arabian serin. The proximity to cultivated areas and to rough scrub is important also for seed-eaters like Philby's partridge. There are signs of junipers at around 1900 metres but they are stunted, looking more like shrubs than the magnificent tall specimens on the western ridge. Whilst most of the rain falls on the westerly side of Sarawat some wadis drain eastwards, their spasmodic flows eventually disappearing into the desert, or occasionally retained by underlying rocks to form permanent or semi-permanent waterbodies as at Wadi Turaba, where freshwater life in the form of fish, frogs, and green algae flourish and yellow cobra abound.

Wadis channel flood waters towards the Tihama plain between the Sarawat and the Red Sea, flowing like torrents when rain falls in the mountains, depositing silts to form fertile soils farmed for coffee, maize, sorghum and mocha coffee. Richly vegetated wadis like Wadi Maraba and Wadi Jaw contain fig trees and great rounded *Ziziphus* whose shade provides a habitat for smaller trees and shrubs including *Ceropegia,* cactus-like *Euphorbia,* pink flowering *Adenium arabicum* and the milkweed *Caralluma ruseliana* with rotten smelling flowers attracting flies for pollination. The distinctive *Adenium,* smooth trunk tapering markedly from the base up, may reach 3 or 4 metres in height in these wadis of the southern Tihama whilst it is also found much higher in the Asir mountains, wedged among rock, where it seldom exceeds 50 centimetres. Shunned by livestock as a result of its toxicity, the lovely pink flowers are like a magnet to the Nile valley sunbird which uses its short bill to prick at the base of the flower in order to extract nectar. The wadis are also home for shining sunbirds whilst the little grey hornbill may also be seen here.

This hornbill has some unusual breeding habits. A monogamous species, it nests in natural cavities, where the female seals herself into the nest by partially walling up the entrance, leaving only a narrow slit through which food may be passed. Building the wall from the outside at first, using mud to create the structure, she later mixes her own droppings with bits of food to complete the edifice when she is holed up inside. The male brings food to the slit where it is taken up by the female and either eaten herself or fed to the chicks. These are born naked and blind but very soon develop long legs so that they too may beg for food through the slit, and can raise their backsides in order to squirt their droppings from the nest which is kept clean by the mother. Once the chicks are feathered and half grown the female breaks out of the nest and assists the male in gathering food for her clutch. In order to maintain their insulated and protected home, the chicks now reseal the nest, using their own droppings, and remain there until they are ready to fly; which they do, without faltering, the minute they depart from the nest.

Undoubtedly one of the rarest plants in Saudi Arabia occurs in alluvial soil at a secret location on the lower section of the Sarawat escarpment, along the side of a wadi. There we find just 16 trees belonging to the species *Mimusops laurifolia,* the only ones left standing in the whole of Saudi Arabia. The wadi where they are found, like other wadis along the escarpment, was once covered by dense evergreen woodland and the isolated groves of *Mimusops* are the last remnants of this ancient plant community with its strong African affinity.

Two of the most important wadis which drain waters from the Sarawat are the adjacent systems of Wadi Juwah and Wadi Dahim which converge into Wadi Gizan, now dammed to create a major reservoir. The complex of wadis through which the waters flow is known as Hakima, and is renowned for its wildlife, particularly its Afro-tropical elements. Wadi Jizan, dammed to create a reservoir of 70 million cubic metres, has submerged several wadis to form an exceptional wetland habitat, important for resident wildlife and as a resting and feeding area for migrating birds following the Arabian fly-ways to and from Europe. Here, for example, one finds a relict population of guinea-fowl, the only significant population of the species remaining in Saudi Arabia.

Within the Tihama foothills, through which the wadi system flows, four major ecosystems have been identified: (1) *steep slopes,* dominated by drought-resistant lowland deciduous woodland such as *Acacia tortilis,* other acacias and the distinctive flamboyant *Delonix elata* tree with its large umbrella of creamy flowers blossoming in spring; (2) pediments, usually sparsely vegetated, and again dominated by *Acacia tortilis* but accompanied here by characteristic shrubs like the flaming bush *Anisotes truculus,* an Arabian endemic woody perennial covered with bright orange flowers and dark green leaves (attractive to many birds as nesting sites); (3) basins, dominated by evergreen woodland formed by the drought-resistant tree *Dobera glabra* with its toughened leaves, and other trees such as *Ziziphus spini-christi* and *Acacia ehrenbergi*; (4) and finally the wadis, dominated by dense stands of Tamarix trees, tall grass and several shrubs including the broombush, *Leptadenia pyrotechnica,* so named for its use by the Bedouin as a favourite source of firewood.

Two hundred and thirty-three bird species have been recorded by

NCWCD biologists at the Wadi Juwah/Dahim systems. The vast majority of these were in some way or other associated with the large lake area formed by Wadi Gizan Dam. The list includes locally breeding species, summer visitors, passage migrants, winter visitors and vagrants. The large number of recorded species emphasizes the tremendous importance of this region for wildlife in general and birds in particular. Among mammals found in the same region are six species of bats, the Ethiopian hedgehog, wolf, red fox, white-tailed mongoose, genet, hyena, wild cat, hyrax, Cape hare, spiny mouse, Baluchistan gerbil, and hamadryas baboon. In addition, ten snakes, ten lizards, an endemic turtle, two amphibians, and an endemic freshwater fish have been found there.

The valley of Wadi Juwah seems more African than Arabian, an effect enhanced by the beehive huts of the human inhabitants as well as by the African elements of its wildlife. It is only here that the Arabian guinea-fowl (*Numida meleagris*) survives. Recently identified as a uniquely Arabian sub-species, it is smaller than its African relative and has fewer spots. It has no head feathers but a bony crown that helps to keep its brain cool. It feeds off the villagers' sorghum crops. However, guinea-fowl do not breed in the sorghum but will only lay their eggs in scrub patches at the edge of the field where the cover is sufficiently dense. The expansion of agriculture which is reducing this cover, combined with the large number of feral dogs who attempt to feed on the chicks, form the greatest threats to its survival. A survey carried out in 1988 put the number of birds at around 350 and it is now thought that conservation efforts will lead to an increase in the local population. Since the birds nest on the ground and have a very high juvenile mortality in the wild, they lay large numbers of eggs. Artificial rearing of these has been adopted as a means to build up the population. There is particular local pride in this unique population of guinea-fowl which are protected from hunting by a local decree.

Despite the development of local agriculture and the relatively dense settlement of the valleys there seems to be a greater appreciation for wildlife here than in some other parts of the peninsula. Agriculture has developed at a gradual pace, using traditional methods of drainage channels for irrigation and, until recently, ploughs pulled by bulls rather than tractors. Fields are flooded by damming channels, a process which deposits fertile silt as well as watering the ground. Although the fields themselves are cleared of natural vegetation, it is encouraged around their perimeters where large *Dobera*, fig and *Ziziphus* trees provide fruits and leaves as food for livestock, shade, and a renewable source of timber. The greatest threat to survival of this ancient woodland is over-grazing of the undercanopy by goats or sheep which remove young seedlings preventing replenishment of natural vegetation.

Wadi Gizan, like other major waterbodies in Arabia, has attracted a wide range of birds including many species of national and international importance such as large raptors, cranes, waders, herons, ibis, bitterns. The high concentration of species in such a small area offers unique opportunities for ornithologists. It has become a freshwater nesting site of immense ecological value as it is one of the few freshwater nesting sites on the long migratory path between Eurasia and Africa.

Strangely enough one of the densest regions of woodland after one leaves the Sarawat escarpment and descends onto the Tihama coastal plain, occurs right at the edge of the Red Sea, half in and half out of the water. Mangroves, primarily *Avicennia marina,* form impenetrable thickets of greenery and are themselves important nutrient-recycling ecosystems supporting a rich variety of invertebrate and vertebrate life. They are a sharp contrast to the adjacent parched earth of the low-lying land between the mountains and the sea. Vegetation on the Tihama itself is restricted to some salt-loving, typically coastal plants such as *Salicornia, Arthrocnemum,* or *Halopeplis* and desert shrubs like broombush. The main tree standing here today is the hardy acacia, *Acacia ehrenbergiana.* Towards the southern Tihama there are also thickets of *Salvadora persica,* the occasional *Balanites aegytiaca* as well as the wild doum palm (*Hyphaene thebaica*) and cultivated date palms (*Phoenix dactylifera*). Across the hot and dusty plain Egyptian vultures and black kites keep a sharp lookout for available food. In spring and autumn the Tihama forms an important migration route for millions of birds on their north or southward journeys and many rest in bushes such as those of *Salvadora,* which provide almost the only cover. Few of the floods in the wadis make it right across the Tihama before drying out but wherever water is present one finds heron, waders and spoonbills.

South of the Asir mountains in the south-west corner of Saudi Arabia, the southern Sarawat escarpment extends into Yemen. The highest peak in all Arabia is found here: Jebel Al Nabi reaching 3666 metres. Despite its superior elevation it is not the most dramatic of Yemen's rugged mountains since it is but a slight rise from the highland plateau rather than a sheer mountain at the edge of the escarpment. Approaching Jebel Al Nabi from the east in a four-wheel drive vehicle it is actually possible to reach the summit.

The escarpment edge further to the west only reaches around 2600 metres but it is more impressive with peaks such as Jebel Melhan and Jebel Bura towering over the Tihama plain. Along the steep slopes of this relatively high rainfall area vegetation and wildlife flourish and woodland thrives, even as low as 500 metres. The peaks have greatly benefited from their isolation but lower down the slopes and in more accessible parts of the Yemen highlands the land has been intensely cultivated or grazed for millennia. Indeed, this section of the peninsula has long constituted the most populous region of rural Arabia and its inhabitants have perfected the great art of irrigation. The first Europeans to investigate Yemen's botanical riches were Peder Forskål and his fellow members of the Arabia Felix Expedition which came to Yemen in 1763. Forskål died of malaria and it was left to his friend and colleague Carsten Niebuhr to ensure that at least some of his collection finally arrived back in Europe. The results of his work were posthumously published in 1775. Many species thus described and named by Forskål are supported by inadequate original material against which modern biologists may check plant characteristics. The scientific interest is further heightened by the fact that many African plants were first encountered by Forskål and his colleagues here in Yemen, and their species derivations are thus based on Arabian material. As we have already seen, this region of Arabia lies at the meeting point of African, European/Mediterranean and Oriental species and there is also a high level of endemism, so our interest in plant and animal life of the Yemen mountains is no less acute today than it was in Forskål's time.

The natural vegetation and wildlife of the Yemen mountains is similar to that of the Asir except that there are no juniper forests here. However, even though *Juniperus procera* does not form woodland, reasonable quantities of juniper do still occur in the Yemen highlands, for example at Kawlan al-Sham, Jebel Lawz, Jebel Sawraq and the Hoogariah. It is usually found in association with olive trees and *Dodonea viscosa*, above 2000 metres, but not at extreme elevations. In the past it seems to have been a characteristic of the lower rainfall areas (250–600 millimetres) at highest altitudes. Further down the slopes, at around 1500 metres, the ancient vegetation pattern was dominated by a form of African savannah type of country in which *Acacia tortilis* and other acacias were the main trees. Beneath the acacia zone there were, and still are in many places, *Euphorbia* thickets formed principally by low euphorbias only a metre or so in height and also by two tree species: the candelabra euphorbia *E.ammak* and *E.pauciramulosa*. Euphorbias in particular are limited in their upward extent by the frost line. The candelabra euphorbia is common in the cloud zone (1600 to 2000 metres) where it may reach 5 metres in height and is populated by golden-winged grosbeaks. The fleshy toxin-secreting leaves and branches of the euphorbias deter many plant-eaters. Beneath the euphorbias, at less than 1000 metres, the mountain plains were probably once dominated by *Tamarix nilotica* and open acacia woodland. The eastern side of the Yemen mountains is too dry for any woodland to survive.

Yemen's varied topography and rich vegetation supports an interesting range of bird life. Raptors such as griffon vultures, barbary falcons, and even the occasional lammergeyer vulture, nest in the high cliffs. Above 2000 metres, along the drier eastern side of the escarpment, the Yemen serin is found in areas of relatively little vegetation. The Yemen linnet also prefers high ground, generally above 2200 metres, and is seen on rocky slopes where vegetation is sparse but not completely absent. Lower down, in the wadis, many of the birds have African affinities. Here for example one may find Rüppell's weaver nesting in *Ziziphus* trees, together with hammerkops, little grey hornbill, Abyssinian roller, shining sunbird and Bruce's green pigeon. Out on the rocky hillsides the fauna includes little green bee-eaters, great grey shrikes, foxes, hares and hamadryas baboons. Below 1400 metres towards the foothills, one may encounter grey-headed kingfisher, black bush chat, African silverbill and, most importantly of all, the last surviving Arabian bustards on the entire peninsula. Even in this remote region this species is extremely rare, perhaps as few as 30 breeding pairs. Nevertheless, they can be remarkably conspicuous, the males displaying at prominent sites, or *leks,* where females can see them clearly as they fan their tails, inflate throat pouches and make strange popping calls.

The northern section of the Sarawat escarpment forms the considerably drier and consequently less enticing Hijaz mountain range. One explanation for their reduced rainfall lies in the fact that they are out of range of the south-west monsoons and are not as high as the Asir or Yemen mountains, thus benefiting less from moisture rising from the Red Sea. Although the vegetation here is generally less prolific than that of the southern Sarawat, the higher summits, such as that of Jebel Warjan, rising 2300 metres above the gravel plain, do have juniper trees. On some mountainsides impressive branching euphorbias are wedged between large boulders: the cactus-like appearance of these succulents suggests a landscape reminiscent of the American wild west! Although the euphorbias appear to be sufficiently well armed with needle-sharp spines which ought to discourage any potential grazer one cannot help noticing that many of them have large chunks torn off their sides. An early morning vigil revealed the culprit – hamadryas baboons living here at the northern extreme of their range.

Among the larger mammals of the Hijaz mountains are idmi or mountain gazelle which still live among the foothills but are more common in the remote stony deserts or *harrats*. They are well-adapted arid dwellers able to survive without drinking fresh water. In addition, the wolf occurs here, albeit in small numbers.

For the past 30 million years Arabia has been moving away from Africa. Upon contact with the Iranian edge of the Asian plate Arabia folded beneath Iran to force up the Zagros mountains. The same forces produced Oman's eastern Hajar range: a series of towering rugged peaks curving around the Gulf of Oman coastline, from Ras Musandam to Ras al Hadd. At Ras Musandam a dramatic limestone promontory rises to 1500 metres and its sheer face plunges directly into the sea. The coastline in this area of Oman is fjord-like with long deep inlets, protected by steep-walled cliffs: an effect created by the mountain gradually sinking back and erstwhile river valleys becoming inundated by the ocean. The largest of these impressive drowned troughs is Elphinstone Inlet at the head of the peninsula. It is 15 kilometres long, 500 metres deep and walled in by cliffs over 1000 metres high in places!

The Sumail Gap divides the Hajar range into two parts, western Hajar dominated by the peaks of the 'Green Mountains', Jebel al Akhdar, reaching 2980 metres, and the somewhat lower, eastern 'Black Mountains' of Jebel Aswad, attaining 2050 metres. These Hajar mountains, like the Asir, receive their moisture from three primary sources: the Mediterranean airstream, north-east monsoons blowing off the Arabian Gulf, and south-west monsoons carrying water inland from the Indian Ocean. Water is deposited in the mountains, as precipitation in the form of rain, hail or even sometimes snow, or else as condensation in the form of dew. The highest peaks of the range receive about 400 millimetres of rain per year.

Despite their name, the slopes of the 'Green Mountains' are devoid of vegetation in many places, especially along the southern flanks which are in a rain-shadow so far as the north-easterly monsoons are concerned. Towards the summit however there are stands of broad juniper trees: *Juniperus macropoda,* a different species to that growing on the Sarawat escarpment. On the well-watered upper parts of the mountain the juniper grow up to 10 metres in height and are well spread out whilst on the southern back-slopes they are found clinging to crevices where water accumulates, usually wedged between cracks in the giant slabs of limestone.

Moving down the *jebel,* at around 2300 metres we arrive at the first olive trees and a shrub known locally as *but (Reptonia mascatensis)* together with *nimt (Sageretia spiciflora)* both of which have originated from Asia and are found nowhere else in the peninsula. At 1350 metres we leave the frost line which restricts the upward extension of *Euphorbia* and here we find *E.larica* as the most conspicuous plant on the steep rocky slopes. Still lower, towards the wadis, we come across large bushy *Ziziphus,* numerous acacia and fig trees. Bird life on Jebel al Akhdar's high cliffs mirrors that of similar habitats in south-west Saudi Arabia: soaring Egyptian vultures, kestrels and brown-necked ravens accompanied by diving pallid swift, pale crag martin and furtive Arabian red-legged and sand partridges live and nest at around 2000 metres.

The vegetation pattern of the lower and less moist eastern Hajar mountains, dominated by Jebel Aswad, is, as one might expect, lacking in junipers, favouring more drought-resistant species, and is, in general, more devoid of plant life. However, these mountains of Oman, to some extent less physically disturbed than high ground in south-western sections of the peninsula, harbour unique wildlife. The Arabian tahr, a mountain goat similar to the ibex, is found here and nowhere else in Arabia. The mountains also share fauna with the southern Sarawat, including, for example, the white-tailed mongoose, leopard and idmi or mountain gazelle.

There is one other mountain range in southern Arabia, contributing to the almost complete encirclement of the south and western borders of the peninsula by high ground and helping to make central Arabia into one massive rain-shadow area. The range in question runs along the Dhofar coast of southern Oman for about 200 kilometres. It is highest in the east where Jebel Samhan reaches 2030 metres while the two other main peaks are Jebel Qara (1050 metres) in the centre of the range and Jebel Qamr (1460 metres) to the west. These mountains, despite their relatively low elevation, are remarkable for their extremely lush green vegetation; among the best examples of indigenous forest woodland to be found anywhere in Arabia. The cause of such profusion is directly linked to their position adjacent to the Indian Ocean, and lying directly abreast the path of the south-west monsoon, known locally as the *Khareef*. This moist, maritime, mountain climate has nurtured the development of a unique flora, markedly different from that found elsewhere in the peninsula.

Southern slopes of the Dhofar range, facing into the monsoon winds, are green whilst the northern flanks face the central desert and are mostly bare of vegetation. The coastal upwelling, dragging cooler water from the depths of the ocean towards the surface, causes mists which blow in over the mountains where moisture is precipitated as rain or dew. This water keeps the water-table replenished and at the base of the mountains there are many springs creating permanent pools: important habitats for wildlife. During heavy rainfall, usually in the monsoon season, from July to September, wadis sometimes run like torrents carrying water and alluvial deposits to the coastal plain or into the desert. For the rest of the year seasonal vegetation dies back and the hills turn brown again.

Jebel Samhan, rising gradually from the desert plain and then more rapidly as a near-vertical escarpment, has a drier climate and is less well vegetated. On its rugged eastern slopes ibex are still found. Jebel Qara, on

116

the other hand, rises over the Salalah plain where grassy downs give way to woodland on the edge of the escarpment. On the gentler slopes, above the trees, there is a savannah type habitat formed by long grasses, whilst near the summit a rough scrubland takes over. Jebel Qamr looms right over the coast so there is virtually no intermediate grassland but just a wooded escarpment replaced by scrub on the backslopes.

One of the most conspicuous species on the woodlands of Jebels Qara and Qamr is an endemic tree, *saghat* (*Anogeissus dhofarica*) favoured by farmers as a source of food for cattle. Like other Dhofar endemics, it only carries its rich green foliage during the monsoon season. Several more widespread trees growing here, such as *Calotropis procera,* come into leaf just after the monsoon season has finished. Birds occupying these woodlands exhibit different behavioural patterns compared to the same species in the Sarawat. For example, the golden-winged grosbeak is not especially associated with a particular tree, as it is with the junipers in the Asir. The general moisture regime is such that sunbirds and the yellow-vented bulbul can tolerate drier conditions than elsewhere. This is also an important habitat for the Arabian red-legged partridge which lives on the edge of woodland and grassland.

Wadis draining water off the mountains and into the desert are a particularly important habitat for several endemic plants, such as *Jatropha dhoarica* and *Croton confertus,* and this is also the home of the endemic spiny mouse and the Dhofar toad, a species which also occurs throughout the region, wherever there is water.

Grassy downs on the mountains are covered by the grasses *Themeda quadrivalvis* and *Apluda mutica.* The former covers the summit of Jebel Qara and is much sought after as a food for grazing livestock. Indeed, its origins may be related to earlier clearances of woodland to make way for grasslands. Whatever its derivation, it is an important habitat for numerous birds especially singing bush larks and long-billed pipits.

The drier mountain slopes of the Dhofar range provide the source of that much sought after resin, frankincense. Its tree, *Boswellia sacra,* is common here but rare elsewhere. To obtain frankincense the bark is peeled back and the resin then oozes out of the trunk. When the precious beadlets have hardened they are collected and the tree may be rested for several years before a new harvest is gathered. Local lore states that the best frankincense is found on trees growing close to the desert and in these areas the resin actually falls to the ground around the tree from where it is collected. In ancient times, Mediterranean peoples had a seemingly insatiable desire for incense. This semi-desert area is also home of Verreaux's eagle, sand partridge and mourning wheatear. Further into the desert there are

117

the usual desert larks, such as Dunn's lark and the bar-tailed desert lark. Among the mammals, one may find spiny mice, hares, and rock hyrax. The latter does not need to drink, escaping the heat of the day in holes and emerging early morning and evening to feed on acacia leaves. Predatory mammals in the remoter areas, where disturbance by Man is at a minimum, include wolf, hyena, caracal and leopard.

Along the coastal plain of Dhofar, beneath the mountains, we still find the baobab tree, an African species. It is either a relict of the area's ancient link with Africa or else has been introduced here. Also occurring here is the Arabian endemic tree *Boscia arabica* which has a dark grey smooth trunk and a flat crown. This habitat, reminiscent of the African coastal region, is inhabited by collared doves, African silverbills and is visited in autumn by magnificent white storks on their migration.

Arabia's mountains provide a sharp contrast with the peninsula's extensive deserts. The mountains capture moisture from the wind-blown clouds, creating concentrations of rich natural vegetation and unique wildlife. They are also the most densely populated rural areas of the peninsula bringing Man and wildlife all too frequently into competition for water and land. Knowledge of these mountain environments has advanced considerably in recent years, primarily as a result of studies instigated by Arabian national institutions. Endangered species and threatened habitats have been identified and concern has been shown for their preservation. Much remains to be done but an important start has already been made.

The great tectonic forces which dragged the Arabian plate away from Africa, lifting the western margins of the peninsula to create the mountain barriers, also left a widening trench which was eventually flooded by seawater to form the Red Sea. This long narrow, imperceptibly spreading arm of the Indian Ocean forms the subject of our next chapter.

118

7

Red Sea Rift

To geologists the Red Sea is an ocean. For millions of years its edges have been moving apart from each other just as Europe and America once separated to create the North Atlantic; or Australia, and India, broke away from Gondwana, to form the Indian Ocean. At the current rate of progress the Red Sea could be as wide as the Atlantic in around 150 million years time. The earth, as we now know, has a crust formed by 12 major fragments and the Red Sea is a rift initiated by the separation of Arabia from the African plate. The opportunity to study the process of ocean-making at such an early phase is reason enough for many geologists to focus their attention on the Red Sea. The fact that its central trench contains pockets of muds extremely rich in precious metals has further encouraged geological surveys. We are therefore fortunate to have quite a comprehensive understanding of its geological past and the various stages by which the Red Sea developed from being a small depression in the ancient Afro-Arabian continent, to the deep tropical sea which it is today.

Two hundred million years ago, and for at least 400 million years before that, the entire region of the Red Sea was land above sea-level. The first indications of a major rise in Tethyan (Mediterranean) sea-level and its incursion across the land which later developed into the Red Sea, are found in deposits from around 190 million years ago, in the Lower Jurassic period. Close to the Egyptian shores of the Red Sea, west of the Gulf of Suez, marine fossils of bivalve molluscs and a brachiopod have been found in sedimentary rocks lying on top of sandstones in which a fern is preserved. The sea's spread across Arabia continued throughout the Jurassic, Cretaceous, and Miocene periods, eventually covering much of the peninsula. Eighty-million-year-old marine fossils are found in marls and limestones from the Upper Cretaceous period, not far north of Jeddah in Saudi Arabia. Comparison of 40-million-year-old sandstones near Jeddah with rocks on the other side of the Red Sea near the tiny Sudanese fishing village of Muhammed Quol point to similar origins and their high concentrations of weathered minerals suggest rapid erosion of the nearby mountains took place at this time. An outcrop of basalt in the same region completes the picture for us, indicating that this was a period of crustal movement and uplift.

Land presently occupied by the agricultural community of Wadi Fatima, to the east of Jeddah, was certainly covered by the sea during the Oligocene period, from 38 to 24 million years ago, since marine sediments from a borehole can be easily identified with this period. Fragments of basalt among the shales tells us that the region was also volcanically active and we can easily see the results of major emissions of basaltic lava in northern Egypt, along the Gulf of Suez and Sinai, and in south-west Arabia and Ethiopia. In places, these Oligocene lavas are up to 1463 metres thick. Eruptions along the longitudinal axis of the rift, which today forms the Red Sea, were clearly associated with tension in the earth's crust and the start of major faulting creating the Red Sea depression.

Once the longitudinal crack appeared and a depression formed the two plates began to move apart from each other at a rate of approximately 1.3 centimetres per flank per year. Around 25 million years ago the basin became cut off from the Indian Ocean. The flow of water into the basin from the Mediterranean was for long periods insufficient to compensate for losses through evaporation so that sea-levels fell, accompanied by the deposition of salts. This is reminiscent of what is happening at present in the Dead Sea. Although salt-deposition due to evaporation continued, the process of enlargement was temporarily halted, tectonic movements ceasing around 20 million years ago, after roughly 18 million years of steady separation.

About five million years ago the two plates recommenced their movement away from each other: the most recent phase in Red Sea development. The renewed faulting caused some steep rift-escarpments on each side of the longitudinal 'crack', exposing thick layers of salt which had been deposited during the 'inland sea phase' of the Miocene. Today these are covered by about 2000 metres or so of sea-water, their ancient salts and shales, rich in heavy metals, helping to create the unusual hot brine pools of the Red Sea deeps. Faulting was also associated with uplift of the land, closing the Red Sea's connection to the Mediterranean, whilst to the south the waters of the Indian Ocean gained access to the deepening trough.

The land margins of the Red Sea are bound by 'raised reefs' which are clearly evidence of periods of higher sea-level. These limestone cliffs in Sudan indicate that levels were up to 16 metres higher around 80 000 to

120 000 years ago whereas deposits further north, in the Gulf of Aqaba, were laid down up to 250 000 years ago. Comparable features may be found beneath the surface of the Red Sea where coral-reefs are typically terraced in the form of a shallow reef-flat terminating in a reef-crest at the surface, dropping almost vertically to the first terrace at around 12 metres. This forms a relatively level section of sea-bed between the shallow reef-face and the next 'drop-off' which can plummet from around 15 metres to perhaps 30 metres. A second terrace may occur before a deeper slope takes one beyond normal scuba-diving depths of around 60 metres. Such terraces mark ancient shallow reef-flats whilst the deeper 'drop-offs' were formed by erosion or as 'shallow reef-faces' similar to those found today, from the reef-crest to around 12 metres.

Clear evidence of lower sea-levels was encountered during our filming off the Farasan Islands in Saudi Arabia. While reef-building corals flourish where tropical sea-water is clear due to the low level of dissolved nutrients, and where sediment or large seaweeds do not smother their delicate polyps, in the nutrient-rich southern waters of the Red Sea, seaweeds dominate and the shallow water corals are much less prolific. One consequence is that the ancient form of the coastline has been less disguised by subsequent coral growth than in the central and northern Red Sea. Swimming down a steep wall we were surprised at around 15 metres to encounter a deep undercut at the base of the submarine cliff, strikingly similar in form to the wave-cut cliffs at the surface. It was absolutely clear to us that the sea had once broken along this cliff-face, cutting into the rock, just as it was doing 15 metres above us today at the surface. As I swam through the long wedge-shaped groove, with its ceiling garlanded by orange soft corals and bright red gorgonians, I found myself imagining what it must have been like here 20 000 years ago. I would then have been wading along a wave-washed ledge, splashed by a much cooler sea. At that time there would have been few if any living corals.

These dramatic rises and falls of sea-level over the past million or so years have been associated with a pattern of global climatic variation in which long periods of colder weather have alternated with warmer temperatures. During the cold periods sea-level fell, partly because more water was trapped in polar ice-caps, and partly because the volume of water contracts as it cools. In warmer periods sea-level rose due to release of water from the ice-caps and also due to expansion of sea-water volume as temperatures increased.

The coastal margins of both sides of the Red Sea are indented by various natural harbours known as *mersas* along the African side, or *sharms* along the Arabian coastline. Many of these are in fact drowned river valleys or wadis through which flood-waters once flowed into the Red Sea. The wadi floors are therefore alluvial basins and the depths of these are indications of previous sea-levels. Such features have indicated that fluctuations over the past hundred thousand years or so have ranged between a minimum sea-level of around 120 metres *below* present-day level and a maximum of around 20 metres *above* today's sea-level. Dramatic lowering occurred during the last glacial period when the level fell below the shallow bar at Hanish Sill and once again isolated the Red Sea. As had occurred on several occasions in the past, the enclosed marine basin continued to lose water through evaporation and became steadily saltier. The absence of a regular infusion of nutrients from the Indian Ocean waters also resulted in an impoverishment and rapid decline in marine ecosystems to the detriment of corals and coral-associated organisms.

The net result of this turbulent geological and biological record is that the existing living coral-reefs of the Red Sea are among the youngest in the world, having developed only since the most recent rise in sea-level brought Indian Ocean waters back into the Red Sea and the shallow marine environment once more approached its present status. Whilst the last post-glacial sea-level rise began around 11 000 years ago, optimal conditions for coral growth in the Red Sea were only attained around 6000 or 7000 years ago. The reefs which have grown up since then have done so on top of other older reef-forms and, as we have seen, their development is dictated as much by the underlying structure as by present ecological influences.

Two coral types have exerted their influence, probably more than any others, upon the Red Sea reefs of today: massive, rounded *Porites* form huge coral-heads and 'bommies' along the sheltered sides of reefs, often creating steep drop-offs of 8 to 10 metres from the crest, whilst branching *Acropora* are characteristic of the exposed, wave-washed sides of reefs and may form branching 'staghorn', bracket or large table-like colonies. Present reef-building corals, considering their relatively brief existence in the Red Sea, have been remarkably successful, creating one of the most prolific and dramatic coral environments to be found anywhere. The most recent review of Red Sea corals lists 53 genera and 177 species of which 2 genera and 13 species are regarded as possible endemics.

Before we consider the reefs themselves it is necessary to take a brief look at the basic physical features of the Red Sea as it is now. Bearing in mind the geological record, we must continue to regard the Red Sea as in a state of flux. As we have seen, it is gradually widening (at a current rate of around 4 centimetres per year) and is presently connected to the Indian Ocean via the Strait of Bab al Mandeb. In the context of global warming we should expect an acceleration in rise of sea-level and, if anything, a greater input of Indian Ocean water over the coming millennia. To the north, the Gulf of Suez leads through the man-made Suez Canal, and into the Mediterranean. Whilst there has been some limited exchange of species via this artificial waterway, most movement has been from the Red Sea into the Mediterranean, and virtually all Red Sea marine life originates from the tropical Indian Ocean.

The basin forming the Red Sea is long (1932 kilometres), narrow (from 29 kilometres wide at the Straits of Bab al Mandeb to 354 kilometres between Massawa and the Saudi–Yemen border; with an average width of only 280 kilometres) and, for much of its length, steep-sided. Although its maximum depth is 2850 metres, its average of only 491 metres compared to the general average for the world's oceans of 3700 metres re-emphasizes its recent origins as an ocean in the making. The absence of permanent rivers flowing into the Red Sea has two major consequences: firstly, there is very little fresh water available to counterbalance loss of water due to evaporation; and secondly, the possible replenishment of minerals washed into the sea from riverine sources does not occur. Given these facts, one must look closely at the circulation of water within the Red Sea in order to understand the distribution of marine life.

Most of the Red Sea is quite deep. Slightly less than a quarter of its surface area is in the 0–50 metre range; 17 per cent lies between 50 and 100 metres; 45 per cent from 100 to 1000 metres; 11 per cent from 1000 to 1500 metres and the remaining few per cent is deeper, down to 2000 metres and beyond. In effect, this leaves only the 25 per cent above 150 metres for growth of reef-building corals or other light-dependent life on the sea-bed such as algae or sea-grasses. The significance of this is heightened by the fact that its clear waters (in the mid- to north Red Sea) are poor in nutrients, and productive ecosystems are therefore dependent upon efficient recycling. The Red Sea's algal or coral dominated reefs and its sea-grass beds are havens for invertebrates, fish, turtles and even marine mammals, despite a generally poor nutrient level.

Each spring, as the Red Sea warms up, evaporation of its surface water increases, and the sea-level falls. By mid-summer the level in the central region of the Red Sea has dropped by almost a metre, exposing reef-corals, killing their uppermost polyps, and creating a seasonal inter-tidal zone which will not be inundated again until the autumn. By October the combination of a lower sea-level, and the onset of north-east monsoons, drives Indian Ocean surface water into the Red Sea, across the Hanish Sill, bringing new fertility and heralding an explosion of planktonic life. The current of nutrient-rich water sweeps northwards, through the southern Red Sea, along the edge of the Farasan Bank, and north-westwards towards

Trinkitat Delta and the islands of Suakin Archipelago. Satellite imagery has traced it this far but by this point it has become so faint that its course is no longer detectable.

The effects of this infusion on creatures inhabiting the shallow sea-bed and coral-reefs is electrifying. Fish which spend the rest of the year seemingly anchored to the reef, avidly defending their small feeding patches, fussily picking at one type of attached invertebrate, or boringly browsing on a particular alga, suddenly forget that they are supposed to be coral-feeders, herbivores or reef-predators. As the first harvest of plankton arrives they simply shed their identity tags and join the crowd, forming bizarre mixed schools of opportunistic planktivores, shattering conventional compartmentalization into highly specialized feeding groups.

For most of the year, snorkelling or scuba diving along the shallow windward edge of Red Sea reefs, one encounters shimmering shoals of orange-red, blue-green or black and white planktivorous fish. Each individual swims directly into the current, concentratedly picking at tiny items of plankton as they drift towards the reef. The competition for food is fierce and the temptation to move out that little bit further than one's neighbour is at times both irresistible and highly dangerous. The benefits of obtaining first bite at the cherry are instantly counterbalanced by the increased risk of transformation from predator into prey! Larger reef-associated predators like jacks, snappers and barracuda often hunt along this moving barrage of reef-dwelling plankton-feeders and their imminent approach is revealed by the darting of tiny fish seeking cover among the coral-formed crevices of the reef.

The intensity of this constant battle for food and survival never ceases to impress me. A sure sign of a healthy reef, it serves as a reminder of the importance of the coral-reef itself in forming a trap for nutrients and, like oases in the heart of the desert, a concentrated haven for all forms of life. Were it not for the annual replenishment of sea-water and nutrients from the Indian Ocean, however, the entire process of reef development would cease because of one other oceanographic peculiarity of the Red Sea which I have not mentioned so far. It is the virtual absence (with the possible exception of the northern Gulf of Aqaba) of major upwelling currents. Thus, when organisms from the light-rich productive shallows die, their remains are quite likely to drift down to a sea-bed which is 1 or 2 kilometres deep, and remain there. Deep Red Sea water is particularly low in oxygen, unusually warm, and supports even less life than the upper water-column and this prevents the biological recycling of nutrients and their return to surface layers through vertical migrations of different plankton. That this does not occur to any significant degree re-emphasizes the vital importance

124

of nutrient replenishment from the Indian Ocean.

The Red Sea, as we have seen, has some unusual oceanographic conditions. Sea temperatures at the surface vary from south to north, falling as low as 17.5° Centigrade in the Gulf of Suez in February whilst the southern Red Sea at this time is around 25° to 26° Centigrade. In summer the northern waters have attained the same temperature as the southern Red Sea in winter (26° Centigrade) whilst the south warms further to around 31° to 32° Centigrade. Thus, whilst annual fluctuations of southern waters range through about 7° Centigrade, and in the central Red Sea the range is down to a variation of only 4° to 5° Centigrade, the difference between summer and winter temperatures in the northern Red Sea is 9° to 10° Centigrade. These are mean temperatures and the range of fluctuation can be influenced by local conditions, particularly in the north where cold north-westerly winds can cool surface waters by an extra 5 to 6° Centigrade. In the south, upwelling waters in the Gulf of Aden may also temporarily depress summer surface temperatures. This geographic and seasonal variation in sea-surface temperatures has a profound bearing on marine life. Reef-building corals, for example, have an optimum temperature for growth of around 28° Centigrade. Rates of growth tend to decrease as the temperature rises above or falls below this level. In the central Red Sea conditions for growth do appear to be close to optimum with some remarkably fast rates recorded (for example, 39 centimetres lateral extension of an *Acropora* table in 10 months) whilst temperatures in the far north of the Red Sea are only just within the range of tolerance for reef-builders.

One of the most telling features of the Red Sea's pattern of water movement and of the biological conditions relating to depth is the gradation of temperature below the surface of the water. In most oceans there is a marked decrease in temperature with increasing depth. The change from one temperature to a cooler one is often quite sudden since different water masses are literally floating on top of each other, with warmer less dense water lying on top of cooler water. Many a scuba diver has experienced these sharp thermoclines in which it is possible to position oneself so that from the waist up one feels reasonably warm, whilst the rest of one's body shivers! In the Red Sea there is one major thermocline, defined in physical terms as the level at which the sea temperature is 1.1° Centigrade below surface temperature. The thermocline moves down in winter and approaches the surface in summer. It is least deep in those areas where surface sea temperatures are higher. Whilst in February the thermocline in the central Red Sea may be at 150 to 200 metres depth beneath the surface, by April it has approached scuba-diving depths at 60 metres and from June to August it is at around 30 metres or even shallower, extending into coastal waters. This seasonal movement of the main thermocline is also of vital significance in controlling the movements of many species, particularly some sharks which tend to swim just below the thermocline. The hammerheads of Sanganeb and other Red Sea reefs are a case in point. The prime time for seeing and filming these shy but impressive creatures is May to June, as the thermocline approaches the 30- to 40-metre level.

Beneath the thermocline the temperature gradient slackens and there is a poorly defined layer of sea-water which, instead of continuing to cool with increased depth, gradually merges with the main body of the water column which is remarkably constant in temperature. What happens lower down in the Red Sea was first recorded by Swedish scientists in 1948, but it was not until 1963 that another team of oceanographers recorded deep-water temperatures of 25.6° Centigrade that scientists focused on this highly unusual situation. A year later workers on a British research vessel succeeded in recovering hot brines and sediments extremely rich in heavy precious metals and triggered a major investigation of the deep central gorge where temperatures in the lower brines may exceed 60° Centigrade!

Below 1 kilometre depth (1000 metres) in the Red Sea there is hardly any plankton, and there are no life forms to carry nutrients which sink to this level back to the surface: unlike the situation in major oceans where vertical migrations of planktonic life span a greater depth range. This circumstance has been invoked in the planning of possible sea-bed mining operations, leading to proposals that the 'wash-waste' or tailings from such mining should not be discharged above 1000 metres to reduce the risk of contaminating surface waters. Discharging waste material from at least this depth would also limit the area of sea-bed over which it would settle.

It should by now be clear that the biological richness of the Red Sea is very much dependent upon the inflow of water from the Gulf of Aden, across the Hanish Sill. As we have seen, one immediate effect which would follow the closing of this conduit would be a drop in sea-level by about 2 metres each year, due to evaporation. As happened in the geological past, the recent coral-reefs would then be uncovered and all their marine life would die. As the level continued to drop, year after year, more and more reef would be exposed and eroded, whilst the steady rise in salinity would kill off other marine life. Fortunately, however, we are not looking at a situation where this is likely to occur since the Red Sea is in a process of deepening and widening rather than becoming a closed sea. Unless there is major uplift of the earth's crust across the plate fracture zone, between southern Arabia and Somalia, the life-giving waters of the Indian Ocean will continue to pour through the Straits of Bab al Mandeb, across the 100-metre deep Hanish Sill, and be drawn northwards, into the Red Sea proper.

126

The flow of water into the Red Sea is a little more complex than a river simply pouring in to top up a large lake. The currents are driven to a great extent by winds. From September to June, the north-east monsoon pushes surface waters from the Gulf of Aden northwards. Inflowing water has a salinity of 36.5 parts per thousand, much closer to that of normal oceanic water than the saltier Red Sea water of around 40 parts per thousand. When the two waterbodies meet, the lighter inflowing water floats on top of the saltier, heavier Red Sea water, and, as the former rushes northwards, the flow is partially counterbalanced by an outflow of denser Red Sea water underneath. During May there is a slight lull in the weather, between the south-easterly winds and the onset of north-westerlies, which blow from June to September. As one might expect, winds blowing steadily from the north-west oppose the established north-flowing current and start to push surface waters from the Red Sea southwards. This happens even though the Indian Ocean water is less dense. There is, therefore, more confusion at this stage between the water layers, involving increasing mixing of wind-blown Red Sea surface water with underlying, northward-flowing Indian Ocean water. The north-westerlies simply impose a third surface current on top of the two previously existing currents so that the outflowing current across the bottom is also maintained. In September, at the onset of south-easterlies, the two-tier system of surface inflow and deeper outflow is re-established.

As waters from the Gulf of Aden flow north they soon become more saline and mix with Red Sea water. Current patterns in the main body of the Red Sea are much less regular than those around its southern entrance. The prevailing northerlies, blowing for much of the year, do tend to create a south-south-east surface current, averaging about a quarter of a knot (or 12 centimetres per second) throughout the northern two thirds of the Red Sea, but the southern third, as we have seen, has more pronounced currents. The inflowing waters travel to the north in a gradually diminishing current which is eventually in opposition to the prevailing north-westerly winds of the northern half of the Red Sea.

One reason for explaining in some detail these seasonal water movements is that they have as much bearing on the distribution of marine life as does the climate and fertility of soil for terrestrial creatures. It is quite apparent that the marine environment of the southern third of the Red Sea, being closer to the source of more nutrient-rich oceanic waters, is in the best position to benefit in terms of production. It is not surprising therefore that its waters are greener and more plankton-laden than the turquoise transparent mid- to north Red Sea, nor that the richest fishing grounds occur in this southern sector. As we move from south to north in the Red

Sea the surface waters tend to become cooler and less rich in phosphates and nitrates (with the exception of the Gulf of Suez). The Gulf of Aden inflow reaches approximately 19° North, or a line drawn from Agig in Sudan to Qunfida in Saudi Arabia, and north of this line there is a dramatic change in the nature of surface waters which suddenly become less green, clearer blue, and less nutrient-laden. One parameter which does increase as one moves north is the oxygen concentration of surface waters, since more oxygen is able to dissolve in the cooler waters which are also agitated by waves.

Apart from their obvious effect on distribution of major fishing grounds, these flow patterns make themselves felt in other ways. Large brown algae such as *Sargassum* and *Turbinaria* tend to grow better in the southern waters where hermatypic (reef-building) corals are much less predominant than in the central and northern waters. Sponges and horny corals, less dependent upon sunlight than hermatypic corals, are also more apparent in the greener southern region. The area around the southern Farasan islands supports large numbers of shrimp larvae, whilst the shallows north of Gizan form important nursery grounds, providing the basis for a valuable shrimp fishery. During filming of our marine sequences around the Farasan islands we encountered extensive level areas of sea-bed which were covered by tall stands of the pink soft coral *Dendronephthya*, creating the only relief on the bottom of the sea. Small snappers and the odd grouper lurked between the soft coral branches hunting for fish or shrimps, whilst sharks regularly cruised through the pink forest, weaving between the delicate soft coral bushes. For divers used to exploring the central or northern Red Sea these southern waters hold many such surprises and have quite a unique character.

Nowhere is this profusion of southern Red Sea life more apparent than on the small islands in the Farasan group where nesting sea-birds find safe havens and, despite the arid nature of their terrestrial surroundings, a bountiful local food supply. Brown boobies, Caspian terns, lesser crested terns, white-cheeked terns, bridled terns and common noddies comprise the main breeding species with elegant crab-plovers nesting in burrows on isolated small islands accompanied by many other species. The islands also provide nesting beaches for green and hawksbill turtles, whilst their shallows are favourite hunting grounds for small sharks. In channels between islands, or wherever there is a current, shoals of gill-raker mackerel and other plankton feeders swim and giant manta rays, powered by graceful wing beats, trawl through plankton clouds, mouths agape, scooping up everything in their paths.

The Farasan Islands are formed from fossil coral-reefs, a fact which visitors can easily verify by merely glancing at any of its raised cliffs where

128

The Red Sea was formed when Arabia broke away from Africa. It is the northern extension of the great African rift system. In the Gulf of Aqaba an immense underwater cliff drops to a depth of 2000 metres (previous page). Vertical walls of spectacular coral fringe much of the Red Sea's length and the most populous reef inhabitant is the tiny red anthias (left and above). Countless millions of anthias seek refuge in the coral. Each group attaches itself to a particular coral outcrop from which the fish move out in shoals to feed in the passing plankton (left). Anthias is the smallest member of the grouper family, even large males only reach a length of 15 centimetres. Females outnumber males by 100 to 1 and when a male dies one of the largest females reverses its sex and turns into a male.

The Red Sea is remarkable for the clarity of its water. Surrounded by deserts with few cities and no permanent rivers to cloud its edges, visibility sometimes reaches more than 80 metres. Like that of the great oceans, its water is poor in nutrients and most marine life is concentrated on the coral walls. The humphead wrasse, seen here with the author, is often found on these deep coral walls where it becomes accustomed to the frequent visits of divers and is even prepared to take offerings of food.

Humphead wrasse reach an immense size – the largest ever recorded was 2290 centimetres in length and weighed 190.5 kilogrammes. It feeds on a wide variety of molluscs, fish, sea urchins, crustaceans and other invertebrates.

133

There are two major sources of plankton in the Red Sea. Vast quantities are borne in with the inflow of nutrient-rich water from the Indian Ocean while other plankton is generated by life on and around coral reefs. Currents tend to concentrate the drifting plankton in certain areas and such places are favoured by many of the larger plankton-feeders, such as giant manta rays (right) and even whale sharks.

Aurelia jellyfish are often found banked up in massive groups (above). They are both part of the plankton flow and voracious plankton-feeders. The Red Sea is, however, a difficult environment for many planktonic organisms. For much of its length its clear, saline water is poor in nutrients. Its great depth means that many nutrients trapped by plankton are not recycled in the surface water but are lost as these organisms die and sink to depths where few species live.

Starfish, brittle-stars, feather-stars,
sea-urchins and sea-cucumbers are all
members of the Echinoderm phylum
which is particularly well represented in
the Red Sea.

The pincushion starfish (above) is
typically found in the Gulf of Aqaba in
the northern Red Sea, where it grazes on
the thin, algal turf covering much of the
reef surface. The bright red and white

sea-star Fromia ghardaqana (left)
is a particularly interesting
hermaphrodite, starting life as a male
and later changing to become female.
Other species like the notorious crown of
thorns starfish feed on coral polyps and
can cause considerable damage to large
tracts of the reef. Once thought to be
caused by Man, scientists now believe
such aggregations are natural.

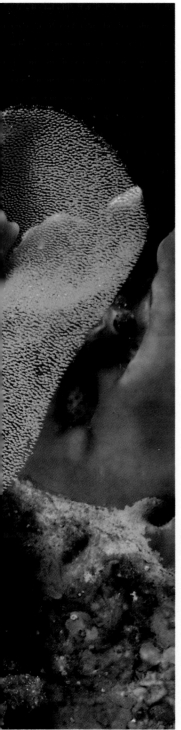

In order that their eggs will survive the
many predators, coral reef invertebrates
have developed elaborate reproductive
strategies that enable their young to find
a safe home for their early development.
One such mollusc is the spectacular sea-
slug known as the Spanish dancer. Both
it and its eggs are avoided by fish because
of their poisonous nature and unpleasant
taste. This protection means it can
deposit its coils of mucus-protected eggs
in exposed locations, such as the coral
outcrop seen below, where they are
constantly washed by water currents and
buffeted by wave surge (left).

140

Ten thousand years ago there were no corals in the Red Sea, the water was too cold and too saline. But, as global seas rose at the end of the last ice age, nutrient-rich water flooded in from the Indian Ocean to renew marine life. Today there are at least 177 species of coral in the Red Sea, 15 of which are endemic and must have evolved as new species since that time. The Red Sea today provides optimum conditions for coral growth. In its clear, deep water, species such as Dendrophyllia (below) can grow to a depth of 300 metres.

There are over 1000 different species of reef fish but few with more successful camouflage than the frog fish (left and far left). Clumsy swimmers, they use their pectoral fins to walk over the reefs where they are easily mistaken for marine invertebrates such as sponges.

Like many reef-dwelling plankton-feeders, fan worms (far left) have an ability both to extend their fan-like nets out into the current to feed and also retract them into strong, stony tubes which are firmly embedded in the reef. At the slightest hint of danger, the fans can be rapidly withdrawn. Most brittle-stars (left) position themselves across the coral surface to feed in the plankton flow. Silneri garden eels (below) anchor themselves in the sandy sea-bed and rise up to pick at the plankton as it drifts by. Spaced a body's length apart from each other, if threatened the entire colony disappears from view, each eel retreating into its carefully constructed burrow.

143

The Farasan Islands in south-west Saudi Arabia were made of coral during a period of higher sea-levels. Today the mangrove bays (right) and coastal inlets are a major breeding zone for many bird species including the endangered sooty falcon and six species of tern, like the bridled tern seen above. The shallow sea between the islands teems with marine life and supports one of the highest densities of osprey found anywhere in the world.

many corals and shells are found in a well-preserved condition. The shallow bank upon which these reefs and islands have developed is supported by ancient salt domes created by Miocene salt deposits pushing up Tertiary sedimentary rocks from underneath. The coastal fringe of many of the islands in the group is inhabited by dense mangroves (the black *Avicennia marina* and the rarer green *Rhizophora mucronata*) which are themselves important habitats for several birds, in particular the goliath heron and other herons which stalk their prey among the aerial roots. The islands are biologically important for a number of reasons, not least of which is their resident gazelle, the true Arabian gazelle (*Gazella gazella arabica*), found nowhere else in Arabia.

Farasan islanders have developed a deep knowledge of the sea and of the seasons affecting its inhabitants. There is an acute awareness of when and where breeding concentrations of fish occur and, in the case of the parrotfish hareed (*Scarus harid*), this has become the basis of an annual festival. In early April each year, as the parrotfish enter shallow waters of Al Qabrh Bay, local people gather at the site, watching for the schools, and then descend on them in droves to frighten them into their nets. The noise and commotion is so great, it seems impossible that any fish could be caught, but when the nets are pulled in they are often too heavy to lift, bulging with ripe parrotfish. Also in springtime, on the island of Qummah, traditional trapping of migratory birds, to be used for food or as a source of cooking fat, also takes place.

Travelling north from Jizan to Jeddah, along the southern Saudi Arabian coastline of the Red Sea, one moves from this region of relatively productive plankton-rich water, beyond the latitude of 19° North and away from the main influence of the Gulf of Aden inflow. The increasing importance of reef-building corals as one moves north is emphasized by the relative absence of fringing coral-reefs south of Al Lith, and their distinct increase north of there. South of Jizan, towards the Yemen border, the only signs of coastal reef development are some very rudimentary reefs formed by red calcareous algae, with occasional colonies of the coral *Siderastrea*, a characteristic south Red Sea species, and dense cover by *Sargassum*. The basic pattern, as one moves north, is one of increasing coral diversity, decreasing coverage by *Sargassum*, and greater development of the fringing reef.

By contrast with the southern Red Sea shores of Saudi Arabia, coral-reefs of its central coastline, for example around Yanbu, are among the most complex and best developed to be found anywhere in the Red Sea. Here, where conditions for coral-growth appear to be optimum, the system comprises a well-developed fringing reef, many patch reefs, together with

145

a discontinuous barrier reef. Interestingly enough these highly developed but very young coral-reefs, less than 6000 years old, are on a foundation of sand and gravel – an alluvial fan washed down from the nearby mountains after the last ice age. Further offshore the reefs are probably resting on an old eroded limestone platform formed by earlier reefs. Scientists who studied coral communities in this region were surprised at the abundance of living corals and the variety of corals found here, comparing them with major Indo-Pacific reefs such as Australia's Great Barrier Reef. Where water movement is strong, branching stagshorn, bracket and table *Acropora* corals predominate whilst massive rounded colonies of *Porites* take over along the more sheltered back-reef. North of Yanbu the Wedge Bank forms a huge area of reefs and islets where corals and associated marine life create some of the most impressive underwater scenery to be found anywhere in the world.

Reef-building corals differ from other, non-reef-building forms in one important respect. The reef-building species all have symbiotic algae or zooxanthellae living within their tissues which greatly enhance the efficiency of their metabolism and enable them to harness the same basic energy source as plants do on land, i.e. light. The obligatory association between reef-building corals and these zooxanthellae thus restricts the vertical distribution of reef-growth to the well-illuminated shallow depths, which in the ultra-clear waters of the central to northern Red Sea and Gulf of Aqaba means down to around 65 metres or so. Corals, extracting calcium from the water and depositing skeletons of calcium carbonate to create the structure of the reefs, grow best from the surface down to around 25 metres, and it is here that the reefs are at their most prolific.

There are many other differences between coral-reefs in various areas of the Red Sea, too many to describe them all in these pages, but the important point which the above comparison makes is that environmental conditions fluctuate within the sea just as much as they do on land. We are too apt to ignore this aspect as we travel across the surface of the sea, unaware of whether we are moving across zones of marine volcanoes, steep mountains, deep valleys or vast plains; or of the oceanographic factors affecting marine life. It is easy for us to appreciate such variation on land and our thoughts on wildlife conservation are often guided by an appreciation of local environmental differences, sometimes quite subtle in their degree, and of the importance of saving particular habitats or a particular species. Unfortunately, much of our thinking about the sea takes place in a more general context and we often fail to realize the uniqueness of a particular marine site.

Scuba diving and underwater photography have changed much of this,

146

particularly with regard to the Red Sea which is enjoyed by large numbers
of divers. As a direct result of increased familiarity with the Red Sea's
underwater environment we have started to recognize sites of special
scientific interest, species under threat, and areas of sheer beauty which
deserve our particular efforts at preservation.

I recall, very clearly, my first impressions of skin-diving in the Red Sea.
I had waded out across a shallow lagoon and over a narrow reef platform
to the crest of the reef. There I was able to stand in ankle-deep water and
look almost straight down, through sea so clear that the brightly coloured
parrotfish and shoals of red jewelfish appeared to be in flight through the
air rather than finning their way through water. The impression was
reinforced as soon as I put my mask in the sea and pushed off with my feet,
launching myself over the cliff edge and into the blue. Now, if I looked
straight down I could see a reef terrace 30 metres below me and if I looked
back at the cliff I was alarmed at first to see how steeply it dropped away
from the surface, overhanging in places, creating shaded sections of wall
or even small caverns. My breath quickened as I took in all this, adjusting
to the fact that I had invaded a world about which I knew very little and
which seemed to be inhabited by every conceivable kind of creature. I took
my first deep breath and dived down a few metres to gain a different view
of this fascinating, and for a while frightening, marinescape. Holding my
position by gripping the base of a small coral I took another look at my
surroundings and gained a different impression. From out of the water the
reef had seemed quite alien; floating at the surface I had been mesmerized
by its beauty and awed by its dramatic form, but now for the first time I
had the sensation of becoming part of the undersea world, a world which
was no longer strange or threatening but colourful and captivating. Today,
years after these first experiences, I am still just as excited when I dive in
the Red Sea, never sure of what I will find there, and never tiring of
studying its unique marine life. As my knowledge of invertebrates and fish
has developed so has my appreciation of the intricate web of life spun by
the corals.

Like everyone else who dives in the Red Sea I am always impressed by
the superabundance of life on the reefs. Every nook and cranny seems to
harbour a fish, shell, crab, seastar, or some other form of life. Hundreds of
fish flash in front of one's face-mask. It would be hard to imagine a more
vibrant ecosystem and yet, just a few yards away from the reef, the waters
are seemingly as devoid of life as the sands of a desert. The Red Sea, as I
have already commented, is generally poor in nutrients and its clear blue
waters do not support large stocks of commercial fish. The illusion of great
richness is created by the tremendous concentration of life around the reefs

themselves and the key to this lies in the reef's capacity to utilize light energy, to trap nutrients, and in the efficient recycling process which occurs.

Everything living on the reef forms a part of this picture. Each organism has a vital part to play and, despite the great abundance of life, the ecosystem is highly sensitive to disturbance or change. At the same time it is a dynamic system in which change forms a vital element in the natural development of the reef. Marine plants and animals are as affected by the seasons as are their terrestrial counterparts. Many Red Sea fish spawn in spring or summer. They do so not once, twice or even on a few occasions, but for hour after hour, day after day, week after week and even month after month. It seems that the chances of an egg being successfully fertilized and surviving to become an adult are very low indeed and the only hope is for a female to produce literally millions of eggs so that a handful might make it to grow into adults. Many times during our filming of the Arabia series, I watched various wrasse, parrotfish or surgeonfish in their special 'mating dances'. The pattern usually consists of a single male fish courting a dozen or more females. The male normally has some means to draw attention to itself, either by taking on brighter colours, extending its fins, or 'flashing' a new shade of colour across its flanks. As the females approach a male pairs off with a single female and they both swim up in the water column, eventually lying alongside each other or with the female tucked under the male. Suddenly their swimming takes on a more vigorous rhythm and each member of the pair emits a cloud of gametes into the water where they mingle and, with any luck, eggs are fertilized before everything drifts apart and before other fish descend upon the clouds, gaily eating the tasty eggs.

In some species the chances of egg survival are enhanced by a less haphazard abandonment of fertilized eggs. Several damsel-fish, highly successful members of the reef community, ensure that their eggs are kept within the reef environment rather than leaving them to drift off in the water column. The sergeant-major (*Abudefdus saxatilis*), a particularly aggressive damsel-fish, glues its eggs to a patch of shallow reef flat where it can tend and defend them. Adults may be seen picking at the egg mats, removing any eggs which are failing to develop, and swimming aggressively at any intruder, rather like gulls or terns protecting their own nests. Another damsel-fish sticks its eggs to the base of sea-whips projecting out from the shallow reef-face.

The question of mating among fish, and of male dominance, has been examined for many Red Sea species but nowhere is the story more fascinating than among the bright red and orange jewelfish (*Anthias squamipinnis*) which forms dense shoals of red plankton-feeders along the shallow edges of many reefs, especially if they are swept by an onshore current. In each shoal there is a single dominant male which rules over many females. The dominant male is slightly larger and deeper coloured than the females and has longer dorsal fin-rays. If another male is introduced to a shoal a fight ensues and the intruder is chased away. This works well for as long as the dominant male manages to keep alive. As soon as he dies, however, the shoal is momentarily leaderless. To fill the gap, one of the older females in the shoal changes its sex, becoming a male, and takes on the dominant role. This incestuous picture is further complicated by the fact that many young males would be unable to enjoy the protection of a shoal were it not for the use of some cunning subterfuge. Rather than incur the wrath of the dominant male and be continually chased away from the shoal, these males disguise themselves as females and are thus accepted as legitimate members of the family. The efforts made by all members of the group to obtain and maintain their presence in the shoal provides some indication of the importance of shoaling as a defensive strategy.

The great value of shoaling is that it enhances the chances of survival for a fish swimming out in the water column, away from the protection of the reef. Not all species are present in such numbers, however, that they can form shoals. One answer to their problem has been to pretend that they are actually members of a shoaling species and thus become accepted by the shoal and also mistaken as one of the group by any potential predator. An excellent example of such a mimic is the mydas blenny (*Ecsenius mydas*) which mimics *Anthias*. The blenny lives in small holes in the reef and may remain looking out from its refuge for quite long periods. Although on close examination it is quite different in shape from *Anthias,* it nevertheless manages to confuse both fish and divers when it swims into the shimmering shoals of jewelfish. Indeed, its mimicry is so good that it eluded discovery until a few years ago and even today few divers notice the mimic among *Anthias* until they have it pointed out to them.

Garden eels employ a different strategy for feeding on plankton whilst remaining safe from predation. Partially extending sylph-like bodies from long tubular burrows on the sea-bed, and curving elegantly to face into the current, they pick at individual plankters drifting by. When danger approaches, whole colonies, often comprising hundreds of eels in a small area, silently and swiftly disappear into the safety of their tubes. Fascinating to watch but exceedingly shy, garden eels are very difficult to photograph or film. To obtain the unique footage of these creatures which was used in our Red Sea film, cameraman Peter Scoones built a special hide and operated his camera with remote control equipment.

Whilst scientific research has revealed a great deal about the biology of the Red Sea, much remains to be learnt. During the course of our filming we were always keen to obtain new and interesting footage of sharks, particularly hammerheads. Apart from the popular level of interest in these large predators and the generally held view that any film of the Red Sea must include sharks, our interest in these elusive animals went much deeper. Despite their large size and relative abundance at certain times of year, scientists were unable to answer our basic questions concerning their life history. We wanted to know where they disappeared to in winter; when they bred; what they were feeding on and the function of their schooling. We knew that they migrated, but did not know along which route or whether hammerheads from Sanganeb in the Sudanese Red Sea swam further north each year into Egyptian waters, or south towards Bab al Mandeb. In short, our information did not extend far beyond the knowledge that they appeared at certain reefs from time to time and tended to remain just below the main thermocline.

Sadly, our understanding of Red Sea ecosystems is lagging behind our influence upon them. Sharks, which few people seem to care about, perform a vital role in the balance of reef-life. Their role is similar to that of the big cats in the savannah-lands in that they scavenge on the sick and unhealthy creatures and so maintain reef health. Throughout much of the Red Sea sharks are fished or caught accidentally and their numbers have declined sharply. Removing sharks or other top predators from a reef attacks the natural balance in ways which we are only beginning to understand. Many scientists have commented that the decline in numbers, or complete disappearance, of sharks from a reef area where they were previously common has been accompanied by a general deterioration in the entire ecosystem. Whether the sharks left because of damage to the system, or whether the damage is only partially related to their going, remains unclear. Unless we take care to protect Red Sea sharks, it may be too late to find out.

Manta rays, from the same group as sharks, possess all of their dignity and grandeur without engendering fear. They are the most graceful of animals, wings spanning 5 or more metres. Peculiar frontal lobes fold around their wide open mouths to create a funnel through which water is drawn before it is forced out across gill sieve plates. Divers dream of meeting manta rays and are willing to travel hundreds of miles for the opportunity to swim with them. To the biologist they remain somewhat enigmatic animals. We know almost nothing about their natural behaviour apart from the little which we have learnt on chance encounters. During the course of our film-making in the Red Sea we were privileged to add one new page to our account of mantas. We already knew that they tended to gather at certain reef locations and chose one of these as the destination for some filming in the hope that we would meet mantas. We were not disappointed but were certainly surprised by what we found there. Mantas were present, not as solitary rays or in just a small group, but in their tens. At one point we had over 40 manta rays in view from the surface!

The real excitement took place when we dived in. Mantas are generally shy animals, quite difficult to approach, but these had no thoughts of timidity. We were able to swim right up to them, to touch them, and to join in their swimming pattern. This was what really fascinated us since the rays were not swimming randomly but in tightly formed circles, one after the other. Moving effortlessly, flapping wing-tips breaking the surface, mouths agape sieving the water column, tiny eyes in a fixed stare, they seemed oblivious to our presence. As each ray in the chain came to the end of an apparently invisible line, it dived down, curving backwards until it was underneath the rear of the chain and surfaced to re-join the end of it. This endless hungry procession continued until one of the rays failed to dive, perhaps feeling that the plankton patch had been well harvested, and swam on with the others following in a long serpentine formation. Eventually one of the line decided that it had arrived at an acceptable plankton patch and began feeding again. The others followed and a new loop was created.

This was the first time that such looped chains had been observed in manta-feeding and we were left to speculate on their significance. We had noticed that some of the mantas had shark bites in their fins indicating that sharks are potential predators. The tight feeding patterns were therefore regarded as a form of schooling for protective purposes and we also felt that the large number of mantas had also most probably congregated for breeding purposes. Every potential answer generated a host of new questions and we were once more aware of how little we really know about the Red Sea's ecosystems. Biological studies by nationally based scientists in countries bordering the Red Sea are helping to further our knowledge and organizations such as MEPA, The Meteorology and Environmental Protection Administration, and the Saudi Arabian National Commission for Wildlife Conservation and Development have advanced the cause of marine conservation so that we may now have renewed hope that these fascinating creatures and vital habitats will be preserved for future generations to study and enjoy.

Arabia's marine environments are even more varied than those on land. In this chapter we have been reviewing some major features of the deep Red Sea. In our next chapter we shall be taking a look at the shallow Arabian Gulf on the eastern coast of Arabia.

8

The
Shallow
Gulf

Ten thousand years ago there was no Arabian Gulf. At that time the Tigris and Euphrates Rivers ran all the way down to the Gulf of Hormuz to empty into the deep Arabian Sea. It was only with the rising of sea-levels at around that time that Indian Ocean water again flooded over the Arabian plains to give the Gulf its present shape. Like the Red Sea, the Arabian Gulf owes its origins to movement of the Arabian plate away from Africa. Whilst on its western side the rift thus formed filled with sea-water and gradually widened to become the Red Sea, to the east the plate collided with the western border of Asia in the region of present-day Iran. In the compression zone along the line of collision, folding took place, throwing up the Zagros mountains and causing a sag to develop in the eastern portion of the Arabian plate. This shallow depression eventually developed into the basin of the Arabian Gulf: a broad shallow valley between the present coastline of Arabia and Iran which has intermittently undergone flooding by sea-water as today, or emerged above sea-level, forming a southward extension of the Tigris and Euphrates delta.

This formation began around 20 million years ago, but the Gulf itself is much more recent, probably around three to four million years old. Since that time it has filled and emptied several times as global sea-levels changed. The Pleistocene was marked by a series of glacial periods in which sea-level fell, followed by inter-glacials when it rose again. In the last inter-glacial, from approximately 125 000 to 80 000 years ago, sea-level in the Gulf was 4 to 5 metres above its present level, flooding large sections of the eastern coastline of Arabia and drowning many of the present islands including most of Bahrain. During the last ice age the process was reversed and sea-level fell so low (approximately 120 metres below present tide marks) that the entire bed of the Gulf formed dry or marshy land through which rivers flowed to meet the Indian Ocean close to the southern entrance of the Gulf at the Straits of Hormuz. Then the global climate once more began to warm and the Gulf returned to a marine environment, tide levels reaching 2 metres above their present height around 7000 years ago and then falling to around 1 metre higher than today approximately 5000 years ago, before oscillating between this and present levels.

Today the Arabian Gulf forms a shallow extension of the Indian Ocean, 240 000 square kilometres in area, 984 kilometres long with a width of between 56 kilometres (in the narrow Straits of Hormuz) and 336 kilometres. The average depth is only 35 metres whilst the maximum, in a deep channel close to the Iranian coast, is 100 metres. As a direct result the water column is generally very well mixed with no marked stratification of different water layers. The high rate of evaporation resulting from hot air temperatures and brisk winds, inadequately compensated by the inflow of fresh water from the Tigris-Euphrates/Shatt al Arab waterway to the north, causes high salinity. In shallow bays where water exchange with the main Gulf is restricted, this saltiness can climb to intolerable levels, eliminating all but the most resilient forms of marine life.

A second effect of the Gulf's shallowness is that temperature fluctuations at the surface, caused by heat radiation or by rapid evaporative cooling, are transmitted throughout the water column, influencing all marine habitats. In most seas or oceans these effects are dampened by a great reservoir of deeper water. The Gulf's strong winds ensure that the water column is very well mixed and this means that diurnal or seasonal temperature fluctuations are felt by organisms on the sea-bed almost as much as those in the shallows. In fact the seasonal variation in sea temperatures of the Arabian Gulf are very dramatic, summer temperatures along the Saudi Arabian shoreline reaching a tepid 35° Centigrade whereas they drop to a really chilling, too cold for comfortable swimming, 10° Centigrade in winter.

Like the Red Sea, the Arabian Gulf's southern connection to the Indian Ocean is through something of a bottleneck, restricting water exchange and greatly limiting the potential of the Indian Ocean to buffer salinity and temperature extremes. At the Straits of Hormuz there is an outflow of saline and heavier Gulf water across the sea-bed and an inflow, near the surface, of lighter Indian Ocean water. Unlike much of the Red Sea however, the Gulf does experience significant diurnal tides and these create currents and promote water exchange rates which are important factors in marine productivity. Tides are also responsible for the existence of an 'intertidal' zone which, as we shall see, is remarkably rich in both variety and abundance of organisms.

Despite the fact that the Arabian Gulf supports some important ecological zones and commercially valuable fishery resources, one cannot escape the fact that many of its inhabitants are, at one period of the year, living close to their tolerance limits with regard to salinity or temperature. This is one of the features which makes the Arabian Gulf of such biological interest.

The Gulf's marine environment can be conveniently separated into two basic categories: the intertidal and subtidal zones. Within the intertidal there are a variety of shores ranging from sheltered mud-flats to sand-flats, sandy beaches and rocky platforms. Most of the coastline is very low and the intertidal zone is often quite extensive, sloping gradually to low-water mark. Where the coastline is exposed to direct wave action, the adjacent shallows often extend for quite a distance offshore and waves break long before they reach the beach, diffusing their energy across the shallows. The beaches themselves may be formed of white carbonate sand derived from broken corals, shells and other marine organisms. In places, wind-blown sands, dark in colour, tending to be yellow or reddish, mix with the lighter marine sand or form adjacent dunes. However, most of the sand-dunes along the Saudi Arabian shoreline are formed from marine carbonate sands rather than those transported by the wind from the surrounding deserts. Their sand-grains may be bound to a greater or lesser extent by vegetation which can tolerate a salty environment such as the beach-grass *Halopyrum mucronatum*. Lower down, in the true intertidal zone, the sand-grains are continuously shifted by the tides and turned over by organisms dwelling there. The ghost crab (*Ocypode saratan*) is one of the most conspicuous shore creatures, building its burrows close to high-tide mark. Voracious nocturnal feeders with catholic tastes, one of their favourite food items is young hatchling turtles whose parents nest on these shores. Ghost crabs are particularly evident during the breeding season when males erect high sand pyramids to alert females to the location of particular burrows. Having mated within these specialized structures, males return to their single-tenant homes after about a week.

In a recent study of the intertidal zone on the Gulf's sandy beaches 400 000 organisms, belonging to 147 species, were discovered to be living in each square metre of beach. Aramco biologists have actually found over 200 species of macrofauna on Saudi Arabian exposed sandy beaches, underlining their biological importance. Steeper beaches had less fauna and habitats close to industrial projects tended to have the lowest diversity. The study underlined the susceptibility of the Gulf's shore life to oil pollution.

Rocky beaches in the Gulf are often formed from calcium carbonate beach sand, dissolved by slightly acidic fresh water, washing down in

154

solution to the water's edge where the alkalinity of sea-water solidifies it into calcium carbonate or limestone. These platforms of beach-rock may be broken by wave action into limestone slabs and smaller rocks creating a rocky shore which provides anchorage for weeds, and crevices for oysters, mussels, barnacles or clams. In many places rock is derived from the erosion of a raised limestone beach extending inland from the top of the shore. Wherever there are rocks in the upper shore these tend to be blackened and this is often mistakenly ascribed to oil pollution. The agent is not oil, however, but blue-green algae which coat the surface of rock in a narrow band, also boring into it, weakening its structure and hastening erosion.

The most conspicuous crab on Gulf rocky shores is *Metopograpsus messor* which scuttles sideways over the algal-coated boulders, scraping for food. A crustacean packing a particularly powerful punch is the mantis shrimp (*Gonodactylus demanii*) which is able to stun its prey, or even to shatter the shells of small molluscs, with a single blow of its front claw. The pistol shrimp, *Alpheus,* also found under stones of the intertidal area, has a similar technique for capturing its dinner.

The most productive area of the Gulf's shores are the extensive tidal flats, many of which have been filled in as part of coastal development and land reclamation. A band of salt-tolerant plants such as *Arthrocnemon macrostachyum* and *Halocnemon strobilaceum* frequently fringe the upper edge of these flats where the mud surface is often riddled with holes made by the crab *Cleistostoma dotilliforme* which is the main species of macrofauna found here. On the seaward side of these flats one often finds dense stands of *Avicennia marina*, the black mangrove. From around the base of these trees long lines of aerial pneumatophores radiate out across the mud, providing a means by which buried roots can breathe since the deep mud is quite deficient in oxygen. Mangrove thickets are important sediment and nutrient traps, supplying nursery areas for fish and shrimps.

Next in succession, as one moves out across the tidal-flat, is the algal-mat zone, an area in which the sediment is consolidated by a mat of blue-green algae and diatoms. The algae furnish both food and concealment for many small organisms, especially tiny gastropod molluscs, microscopic crustaceans and worms. Crabs are not nearly as plentiful here as elsewhere on the shore since the algal mat tends to prevent burrowing. Moving to the seaward side of the algal mat zone one encounters an area of very liquid mud which is favoured by the burrowing crab *Macrophthalmus depressus* and is consequently referred to as the *Macrophthalmus* zone. At low tide the crab stands just outside the entrance of its burrow sifting organic material from the sediment. Closely related to fiddler-crabs (belonging to the genus *Uca*)

155

Macrophthalmus exhibit a somewhat similar claw-waving behaviour in which males beckon to females or threaten other males by gesturing with their large blue front claws.

Seaward of the *Macrophthalmus* zone, and down to low-tide level, the mud is dominated by millions of the tiny snail *Cerithidea* which also gives the zone its name. This gastropod is scattered over the surface of the mud in huge numbers, counts of 1000 or more per square metre being the rule rather than the exception.

There are variations on the above arrangement, depending on whether the underlying layer is mud, sand or rock. At lower levels of both mud- and sand-flats an extended long red proboscis or probing tongue often reveals the location of the echiuran worm (*Ikeda taenioides*), burrowed in the sediment. On some sand-flats the ghost crab *Ocypode saratan* is found hunting for *Macrophthalmus* which it digs out of its burrows. In the middle section of sand-flat shorelines the small crab *Scopimera scabricauda* can be abundant, sometimes exceeding 100 per square metre. Its feeding method produces large quantities of faecal sand pellets which give the entire surface a patchy granular appearance at low tide.

Northern shores of the Arabian Gulf have some interesting communities, particularly on mud-flats where three species of mudskippers are common. Largest of the three is the herbivorous *Boleophthalmus boddarti,* a species which gives the mud-flats of Kuwait's Sulaibikhat Bay their unique character because of its habit of building territorial boundary walls. In places, the flats are covered by an extensive matrix of mud walls, creating an almost surreal effect. The mudskippers appear to spend the entire day scooping diatoms and algae off the mud surface or tending the walls. *Periophthalmus koelreuteri,* an amphibious goby, feeds on small crabs whilst the third species, *Scartelaos viridis,* eats plants or animals, probing the mud for anything it can find.

Beaches on offshore coral islands are often selected by turtles as nesting sites. The most frequently observed turtle in the Gulf is the green turtle (*Chelonia mydas*), which feeds on sea-grasses. In addition, the smaller hawksbill (*Eretmochelys imbricata*); leatherback (*Dermochelys coriacea*), the largest sea-turtle of all; and an occasional loggerhead (*Caretta caretta*), are found. Turtles congregate during spring and summer near the islands, females climbing laboriously ashore at night in order to dig a nest in the soft sand and deposit their eggs. Green turtles mature at approximately six years old and nest every two to three years. Since the main sea-grass beds which comprise their feeding areas are some distance away from nesting islands the act of breeding is associated with definite migrations. Once the female has arrived at the nesting area she remains in the vicinity for about eight weeks, returning to the beach in order to deposit new clutches of eggs approximately once a fortnight. Eggs buried under the sand by the female are left on their own to hatch after about 50 days. Baby turtles clambering up through the soft sand to make their way back to the sea act as a signal to attack for every possible predator, both on land and in the water, and many turtles perish within minutes of exposing themselves on the sand. Before they reach the sea they may be eaten by ghost crabs, hermit crabs or by sea-birds. Once they arrive in the water their problems are far from over for awaiting their arrival are groupers, barracudas and snappers. Although many eggs do hatch, the chances of a hatchling making it through to maturity are less than 1:100 and in view of the fact that turtle numbers have been declining, with several species on the verge of extinction, biologists have begun to look at ways of increasing their chances by collecting eggs, raising them in captivity and controlling their release, away from concentrations of predators.

One of the earliest efforts at artificial rearing of turtle eggs taught scientists that it is sometimes better to focus attention on preserving the whole ecosystem rather than seeking to interfere in the delicate balance of nature on behalf of a particular species. The choice can be a hard one to make but turtle biologists in the Caribbean almost caused more damage to turtle populations by artificial rearing than if they had left the turtles to their own devices. What they had not realized was that the sex of a turtle is determined by the temperature of its eggs during incubation. In a natural clutch those on the outside are slightly cooler than eggs in the centre and they become males while those in the middle turn out as females, thus maintaining a balanced population. Even the position on the shore at which eggs are laid can have an effect on the sex of offspring. Those higher up the shore tend to produce more females and those lower down, more males. Without appreciating this sensitive process of sex-determination, biologists carefully collected large numbers of turtle eggs from laying-beaches and incubated them at what they believed to be the optimum temperature. The result, for several years, was that thousands of females were produced and very few males. This seriously upset the sex-balance of the natural population and caused significant damage to future breeding success. It was a lesson in conservation which has made an important impact upon the approaches adopted towards many threatened species. Biologists attached to MEPA and the NCWCD have mounted their own surveys of turtle populations and their biology in the Arabian Gulf. Their efforts will contribute to the long-term preservation of the Gulf turtle population.

Beneath tide-level the Gulf has several important ecological zones which may be classified under two basic types, associated with either hard or soft

157

sea-bottoms. Hard bottoms in the Gulf are formed by coral-reefs, rocks or by artificial structures such as oil-pipes, -rigs or wrecks. Soft bottoms comprise important sea-grass beds, sand or mud. The Gulf's coral-reefs are formed by a restricted collection of corals compared with those of the Red Sea. This is particularly true for reefs near the Arabian shore where environmental conditions are at their most stressful for corals. Here, the combined effects of large temperature fluctuations, high saltiness, and intermittently heavy turbidity and sedimentation make conditions marginal for many reef-building corals. Nevertheless, some reef development has occurred and coral islands have been formed. Not surprisingly, the greatest diversity among corals in the Gulf occurs on reefs in deeper water where there is a wider selection of habitats than on the reefs in very shallow water. On exposed sides of Gulf reefs, *Acropora* species form tables and brackets whilst the reef-tops and sheltered sides are primarily formed by *Porites* and several less important forms such as *Cyphastrea microphthalma*. Brown algae are present on all the reefs with *Colpomenia sinuosa*, *Sargassum boveanum* and *S.latifolium* often occupying more space than corals. On one reef studied in April, *Colpomenia* occupied 90 per cent of the reef-top and *Sargassum* was dominant on the reef-edge, not leaving much space for corals. On most reefs algae seem to gain the upper hand at certain times, particularly in winter, when species such as *Hydroclathrus clathratus* and *Pocockiella variegata* may clog the polyps of live corals, causing them to die. From a biological viewpoint these coral-reefs are especially interesting since they seem to represent the contrary end of the spectrum to those of the central Red Sea where conditions for growth are at their best.

Arabian Gulf coral-reefs are inhabited by quite a wide range of Indian Ocean invertebrates and fish. The massive heads of *Porites* corals provide homes for a variety of boring bivalve molluscs and fan-worms. Branching *Acropora* and *Pocillopora* corals have their fair share of accompanying crabs such as *Trapezia cymodoce* whilst reef crevices host a wide range of sedentary life as well as providing important refuges for reef fish. Among the coral-reef fish of the Gulf there are just three common butterflyfish: *Chaetodon melapterus* which is bright orange with black fins; russet-brown *Chaetodon nigropunctatus*; and *Heniochus acuminatus*. The blue tang, *Zebrasoma xanthurus*, is a prominent algal grazer, whilst several parrotfish, including *Scarus ghobban*, *S.persicus*, *S.psitticus* and *S.sordidus*, augment the fish population. The fish life of the Arabian Gulf's coral-reefs is frequently dominated more by transient visitors like sardines than by typically coral-associated fish. Of course, wherever there is a plentiful supply of small fish such as sardines, predatory species like jack (*Carangoides bajad*) or barracuda abound. Low winter temperatures affect coral-reef fish as much as they do the corals

158

themselves and, since they are much less in evidence during the colder months, it seems that in winter many of these fish either migrate south or offshore, or die.

If the Gulf's coral-reefs survive on the brink, faltering between life and death, its deeper water pearl-beds thrive in the peak of condition and the Arabian Gulf remains one of the best places in the world for the growth of the pearl oysters: *Pinctada margaritifera* and *P.radiata*. The pearl oyster was once the major economic resource of the Gulf region. Entire pearl diving communities migrated in pursuit of these riches and the income from pearl diving acted as the economic mainstay of the people. However, the pivotal role of pearling was replaced by another local natural resource: oil, upon which Gulf states' economies now depend. But the oyster-beds are still there and the pearl oyster continues to flourish in the Arabian Gulf. Its decline in financial importance was dictated by a worldwide recession in the 1930s and by successful marketing of the Japanese cultured pearl.

Pearl oysters have been fished in Gulf waters for at least 4000 years. Small bivalved molluscs attach themselves to a hard object on the sea-bed by means of fine threads. Being filter-feeders, they use gill filaments to sieve the bottom currents for plankton. Once caught, planktonic food is sorted and ingested. The oysters spend most of the day and night feeding, only closing their valves at the approach of a potential predator. The problem of egg fertilization for sedentary animals like pearl oysters is a crucial one. How best can they ensure that eggs are fertilized and hatch into oyster larvae rather than simply remaining unfertilized and providing an attractive food for passing fish? The answer, in their case at least, is for all the pearl oysters on the oyster-bed to release their eggs and sperm into the water column at the same time, thus greatly increasing the chances of fertilization. Following this synchronous spawning, fertilized eggs divide rapidly to become larvae which must feed in the plankton until they are ready to settle on the sea-bed and adopt the life of a young pearl-shell. The planktonic phase, like that of all other marine creatures, is an extremely hazardous one for the pearl oyster and very few of the originally fertilized eggs do make it through to becoming young oysters. For this reason the adult oysters release literally millions of eggs and sperm into the water column. As a result one does not need a large number of breeding adults to produce a heavy settlement of larvae.

The preferred settlement surfaces for young pearl oysters in the Gulf are leaves of the sea-grass *Halodule uninervis*. A single blade of this marine grass may have a hundred or more young oysters attached to it and as these grow they rapidly become too big for the blade to hold, many falling off and attaching to other blades. The main settlement period is in March to April

159

and by October large quantities of dark-shelled young pearl oysters have accumulated on the sea-grass beds before being washed into deeper water where they attach to any available hard foundation and grow into adult oysters. The lustrous pearls for which they are renowned are formed by secretions of the nacreous layer around natural nuclei such as grains of sand which enter the bivalves.

A recent study on Arabian sea-grass beds revealed that annual productivity of *Halophila uninervis* reached 1326 grams of fixed carbon per square metre per year, ranking the beds as among the most productive of the world's marine biotopes. Sea-grasses contribute food to the ecosystem in two basic ways; first, as a growth of leaves which are grazed by specialized herbivores; secondly, through the contribution of dead plant material decomposed by bacteria and fungi. However, despite the high production rates of the plants, relatively few species feed directly upon them and many herbivores prefer to graze on the algae which grows on the leaves.

The importance of sea-grass beds for the Gulf's marine life is reiterated by another invertebrate group whose commercial significance is still a major factor in the local fishery. Gulf shrimps are among the tastiest to be found worldwide and are greatly appreciated by many of the inhabitants of the Arabian Gulf region. The main species, *Penaeus semisulcatus,* breeds in early spring when spawning females discharge thousands of already fertilized eggs into the sea, generally under the protection of darkness. After about 24 hours the eggs hatch into nauplii larvae and become part of the plankton food chain, as both consumers and consumed. Their larvae pass through a series of moults and metamorphic changes to become, first protozoea, then more shrimp-like mysis larvae which gradually take on the form of juvenile shrimps. Young *Penaeus semisulcatus* settle almost exclusively in the algal and sea-grass beds vital for their development, whilst *Penaeus latisulcatus* prefers a clear sandy bottom.

Penaeus semisulcatus shrimps spawn in winter and their young settle, often on thickets of the brown alga *Hormophysa triquetra,* in February to March. They spend only a short while among the algae, however, before moving to the adjacent sea-grass beds, timing their arrival to coincide with optimum spring growth of these marine plants, when food is most plentiful. The young shrimps grow extremely rapidly, their body weight increasing by about 2000 times in only eight weeks. By mid-April to early May many of the juveniles descend into deeper water, joining adults feeding on the sea-bed and in the process become vulnerable to commercial trawling.

The enormous biological richness of Gulf sea-grass beds was emphasized in a recent study of near-shore soft bottom communities. Scientists identified a total of 624 different creatures living on sand or among sea-grasses. Four hundred and fifty-two of these were on sand with 369 among the sea-grasses. A look at the abundance of these creatures in the two habitats revealed a slightly different picture, however, with densities of up to 9670 organisms per square metre on sand contrasting with a maximum of 36 200 per square metre on the sea-grass beds. Apart from turtles, pearl oysters and shrimps, the sea-grass beds play a vital role as a food source for many other animals, including the rabbitfish (*Siganus canaliculatus*), known throughout the region as *safee*, sawfish (*Pristis zysron* and *P.cuspidatus*), several large stingrays and various other fish. They also provide the sole food source for a highly endangered and very shy marine mammal, the sea-cow (*Dugong dugon*), known locally as *arus el baha* (bride of the sea). This is the only living herbivorous mammal which is strictly marine. Related to the now extinct Steller's sea-cow and the manatees of the west Atlantic and Caribbean, the dugong is widely regarded as one of the rarest marine mammals in the world, and great fears have been expressed for its continued survival in the Gulf and elsewhere, throughout its Indo-Pacific range. In times past it was quite abundant in the region and was one of the major sources of red meat for early settlers. Recently, massive oil spills occurring in connection with the Iran-Iraq conflict, and as a result of oil-field or shipping accidents, led biologists to suspect that dugongs may have been eliminated from the Arabian Gulf. An aerial survey was mounted to count their numbers and this led to a surprising discovery of a huge herd of these mammals, containing 674 sea-cows, 81 of which were recently born calves. The herd instantly became the largest known concentration of dugongs to be found throughout the Indo-Pacific and the Arabian Gulf was transformed from its status as a doubtful refuge, to a vital sanctuary for the global population of sea-cows.

Other inhabitants of the sea-grass beds are the greyish-green and black-banded sea-snakes, *Hydrophis cyanocinctus* and *H.lapemoides*. These marine reptiles stalk fish such as gobies or *Plotosus* catfish on the grass-beds, crawling inside burrows in order to reach their unfortunate occupants. Whilst sea-snake venom is extremely toxic to humans, the position of the fangs far back in the jaws doesn't facilitate its injection into large objects, and, since the venom's function is to paralyse prey, unless they are trapped or captured in a net, sea-snakes do not usually attack people.

The Gulf's strong tides have stimulated the development of a unique Arabian fish-trap, the *hadra*. This consists of long lines of poles set perpendicular to the shore-line. These poles guide fish seawards, tricking them into entering a rounded or heart-shaped trap from which they are unable to escape as the tide drops, finally floundering in a shallow pool for easy harvesting at low tide. This method has been used for hundreds and probably thousands of years and was the foundation of the Gulf's commercial fishery before the advent of modern trawling and trapping methods. The *hadra* fish-traps of Kuwait, Saudi Arabia and Bahrain impart an especially Arabian character to their coastlines and uphold a tradition based on harvesting a natural resource in a sustainable way.

As with the Red Sea, not all of the local fish stocks are able to tolerate the pressures of modern fishing and some of the most vulnerable species are sharks. Probably the most common Gulf shark is the bottom-dwelling nurse or cat shark, *Chiloscyllium griseum*. Hiding under ledges during daytime, it emerges only at night to feed on invertebrates, especially shrimps. Among the larger sharks of the genus *Carcharhinus,* the bull shark, *C.leucas,* is the commonest. It grows to about 2.5 metres long and has a broad, blunt head with a large mouth. A strong predator, it attacks sharks and stingrays. Other sharks found in Gulf waters include species like tiger and lemon shark as well as smaller ones like the black-tipped reef shark and the small reef shark. Of these the tiger shark, *Galeocerdo cuvieri,* is the most dangerous and was the most feared by pearl divers. The average size of Gulf-caught tiger sharks is around 4 metres and analysis of their stomachs has revealed that they eat almost anything, from dolphins to large turtles or even other sharks.

The Arabian Gulf is as unique, in its own way, as the Red Sea. Whilst both seas derive their marine fauna from the Indian Ocean their disparate oceanographic regimes support distinct ecological zones. Although coral-reefs do exist in both seas those of the Arabian Gulf are a very poor reflection of Red Sea reefs. On the other hand the Arabian Gulf possesses an extremely rich intertidal zone which is much reduced in the Red Sea where diurnal tides are either small or completely absent. The sea-grass beds of the Arabian Gulf are vital for the existence of many marine creatures, supporting large numbers of young shrimps, pearl oysters, other invertebrates, fish, sea-snakes, green turtles, and sea-cows. The Gulf's marine resources, like those of the Red Sea, have played an important role in Man's settlement of Arabia and continue to be a key source of protein. Modern technologies have also permitted salt-laden waters of both seas to be converted to fresh water suitable for drinking and the sea's resources are being used in a variety of other ways, helping to sustain the burgeoning human population of the Arabian peninsula. The challenge facing all of us is how we can continue to gain from these natural marine resources without literally killing the 'goose which laid the golden egg'!

9

Migratory
Pathways

Every autumn approximately 3000 million birds fly across Arabia. Some of the 200 or so species involved in this great movement remain there for the winter whilst others press on with their journey, eventually settling for a few months in Africa before returning north again to breeding-grounds in Europe or Asia. Arabia is both a land bridge and desert barrier between the three continents: Africa, Europe and Asia. Whilst many birds are able to cross this arid zone on their annual migrations, for others the deserts remain significant obstacles forcing them to avoid the driest regions, or to by-pass them completely. Ornithologists have recently identified major 'flyways' followed by Arabia's avian migrants and have reported some impressive sightings at key bottle-necks along these routes.

Twice a year, in spring and autumn, the Jordanian oasis of Azraq receives a huge influx of temporary visitors, birds belonging to 217 recorded species on migration between Europe and Africa. The oasis forms a migratory focus and an important staging-post where birds can rest for a short time, feed, and drink fresh water. At such times the isolated wetland is alive with the sound of bird song and the wing-beats of duck as they fly in or out of the shallow pools. In spring, innumerable birds arriving from wintering grounds in Africa approach the oasis across a broad front. Studies suggest that many of these have made non-stop journeys from Sudan or Eritrea. Rollers, bee-eaters, kingfishers, wheatear, warblers, swallows, swifts, martins, redstarts, wagtails, pipits, various waders, doves, quail, duck, crane, geese, many other birds, and even swans appear at the oasis for brief recuperation periods, generally lasting for only one or two days. These species are often accompanied by birds of prey such as harriers, falcons, buzzards and eagles. It has been estimated that the oasis, with an area of 120 square kilometres can temporarily support at least 50 000 birds and

163

that the spring migration through Azraq can be confidently placed at several hundred thousand. Many of these migrants continue their southward journey by flying along the western side of Arabia, over the Tihama coastal plain, perhaps guided by the foothills, or by the Red Sea itself, clinging to the shoreline, or following the long ribbon of coastal reefs and islands.

On the eastern side of Arabia, Kuwait lies on the flight path of many birds moving between Europe or western Asia and Arabia or Africa. The spring passage of birds of prey is a major event in the Kuwaiti ornithological calendar, characterized by large numbers of steppe eagles (*Aquila rapax orientalis*) as well as booted eagle (*Hiëraaetus pennatus*), Bonelli's eagle (*H. fasciatus*), spotted eagle (*Aquila clanga*) and imperial eagles (*Aquila heliaca*). The raptors congregate along the edge of the Jal az-Zor escarpment, resting there at night and waiting until the sun's heat has created updrafts into which they launch themselves in the early morning. Riding thermal air currents they spiral higher and higher, eventually taking the 'downhill route', gliding southwards in seemingly effortless journeys towards their destinations. We know that these migrants are heading for southern Arabia or East Africa since birdwatchers have spotted them on their route further south across southern Arabia towards the narrowest crossing of the Red Sea, at the Straits of Bab al Mandeb. There they converge with other birds of prey which have taken the western Arabian flyway, along the Tihama corridor. Steppe eagles, buzzards, short-toed eagles, booted eagles, marsh harriers, black kites and at least 17 other species of raptor pass through the southern Tihama between mid-October and mid-November. In one 15-hour session two observers counted 653 raptors passing along the foothills at Mafraq al Mukhla in Yemen. Most of these (460) were buzzards whilst steppe eagles were also common (173) but less than ten of each of the other species were recorded. On another occasion at least 5000 steppe eagles passed by these foothills. The commonest raptor in North Yemen is the black kite but, as these birds are also resident in Yemen, counts of black kites there do not necessarily mean they are migrating.

Once the two groups of migrants arrive at the Bab al Mandeb straits they tend to remain on the Arabian coast until favourable winds arrive to assist in their sea crossing to Africa. Ornithologists are stationed at two arrival points on the coast of Djibouti in order to complete a count. During a 17-day observation period from 15 October to 1 November in 1985, 61 000 steppe eagles and 17 900 buzzards were logged as they flew in from Arabia, making a first landfall in Africa. By this stage, of course, it was impossible to tell whether the birds had taken the Tihama route or had come down along the shores of the Arabian Gulf via the South Yemen

Hadramawt. At any rate they had arrived, visibly tired but intact. Now they could disperse for the winter months to enjoy the rich pickings of prey and carrion found on the African savannah.

It has been estimated that, during the migration peaks, at least 40 000 birds make this perilous crossing every day. Most of the raptors fly across the Straits between 10.30 and 14.00 hours; clearly influenced by morning thermal currents upon which they rise on the Arabian side before heading west or south-west to Djibouti. Once they have crossed, their route either takes them due west to the area known as Doumeira or else they head south-west to the narrow peninsula and hill of Ras Siyan. The choice is dictated by wind direction since the more northerly destination of Doumeira can be reached by tracking across a southerly wind whilst it would be necessary to fly directly into the wind to reach Ras Siyan in such conditions. If the wind is northerly, however, the birds all head for Ras Siyan; crossing the coast in 'waves' consisting of several hundred flying close together. On departing the Yemen highlands they are at an altitude of around 3000 metres. All the way across the sea they lose height until, at Doumeira, their vertical height on reaching the shore is generally around 50 metres, whilst at Ras Siyan (which makes for a somewhat shorter sea journey) it is still at around 65 metres. Some simply do not make it across and fall short, landing in the sea to be rapidly devoured by predatory fish. As the successful ones arrive, however, they meet new updrafts and ascend once more, spiralling on thermals, eventually drifting inland. In Djibouti in 1985 during a 14-day watch on this autumn migration 81 022 migrant raptors of 22 species were recorded flying across from Arabia. The principal species were steppe eagle (61 119); steppe buzzard (17 900), sparrowhawk (412), short-toed eagle (206), and booted eagle (126).

Whilst these soaring birds are at pains to minimize periods spent over water (where thermal updrafts are considerably less common than over land) this is not a consideration for many of the smaller species which fuel themselves up by eating voraciously before a long flight and often remain on the wing for 1000 miles or more, taking the least obstructed route south. For many, the Red Sea provides a convenient corridor, and large numbers fly along it each autumn and spring. During the course of our filming on the *Arabia* series we spent several months on boats or islands in the Red Sea. Migrating birds were our regular guests on board diving craft or we were theirs on coral islands. During one such voyage, in late October, we were assailed by literally thousands of swallows landing in a state of total exhaustion on board our boat. They were so tired in fact that they cared little whether their perch was the ship's rail or a cameraman's head! Whilst photographing one way-worn swallow alighting on a photographer's head another landed on my camera! If it had not been tragic it would have been very amusing but we were actually aware of the tremendous journeys these tiny birds had accomplished and were anxious to do anything we could to help them survive. We left them undisturbed as they perched on every conceivable surface, and tried to offer fresh water to those not too tired to drink. Each morning we swept up dead birds from all over the boat and we had little faith that those which had taken off again had the strength to go much further. It was clear to us that we were witnessing one of the rarely observed natural tragedies of long bird migrations: mass mortalities of birds caught out for some reason or other, perhaps due to a late departure from Europe, or to contrary winds. Apart from the swallows collapsing on board our boat many thousands more must have been dying in mid-sea. It brought home to us that bird migrations are not quite as clear-cut as we tend to believe.

Apart from large natural mortalities many other migrant birds die through the intervention of Man. One of the small passage migrants to take the Red Sea route is the attractive turtle-dove (*Streptopelia turtur*) belonging to the eastern form, *S. turtur arenicola,* which breeds in north Africa, from Morocco to Libya, in south-west Asia, in Iraq and in parts of the Arabian peninsula. Those using the Red Sea route do so in order to fly between wintering quarters in East Africa and summer breeding-grounds which are most likely in eastern Europe and western Russia. During these autumn and spring migrations the birds rest at many isolated peninsulas or islands and on some of these their arrival is eagerly awaited by traditional bird-trappers. Along the eastern shores of Arabia there are three major dove-trapping locations, at Ras Hatibah and Shuaiba, respectively north and south of Jeddah, and on the island of Qummah in the Farasans. The traps consist of camouflaged netting and mangrove branches, usually adjacent to a natural stand of mangroves. Birds resting among the mangroves are chased out so that they settle on mangrove branches form-ing part of the traps. An earth wall set in the shape of a V tends to funnel birds towards a net tunnel where they are caught in large numbers. It has been estimated that these three trapping stations in the Red Sea account for approximately 100 000 turtle doves each year: more than double the total breeding turtle-dove population in East Germany! Apart from suffering this onslaught the doves are actively hunted in Jordan, Lebanon and Cyprus. Unfortunately turtle-doves are now regarded as a great delicacy causing prices to rise and the pressures on their numbers to intensify.

Like the Nile and Jordan valleys, the Red Sea is a natural corridor with many birds using the sea's edge as a visual flight-path. In spring or autumn one can watch numerous waders, wildfowl, cranes, herons, and exotic flamingoes as they make their way along this route, often flying only a few metres above the fringing reef. A visit to one of the remote islands or lighthouses will be rewarded by close encounters with bee-eaters, hoopoes, kingfishers, rollers, weavers, wagtails, pipits, sooty falcons and a host of other species including some reclusive birds, like the nightjar, rarely seen on land. At the height of the spring migration stunted bushes on Red Sea islands are weighed down by warblers, redstarts, rock thrushes, shrikes and doves. Some of the birds fleetingly encountered on these migrations are endangered species such as the white stork, sacred ibis, peregrine falcon, demoiselle crane, waders and many other species. Their regular appearance across Arabia in quite significant numbers should not be taken as indicating healthy populations since the flyways are restricted and what one is seeing may represent a very large proportion of the total population of a species, rather than a small fragment of it.

One species whose migratory routes have been followed with more than passing interest by residents of Arabia is the houbara bustard (*Chlamydotis undulata*). In the traditional life of the peninsula, prior to the discovery of oil, the houbara occupied a position of great importance as a source of food hunted by Arab falconers. Whilst the houbara is a resident breeder in Arabia, every winter its numbers were vastly augmented by birds moving into the peninsula from Asia. One of the most perceptive Westerners to describe this much celebrated event was H. R. P. Dickson who wrote in his book, *The Arab of the Desert,* published in 1949:

167

> The *hubara* appears on the eastern and north-eastern seaboard of the Arabian Gulf in about October in each year, and birds continue to come till about April, when they gradually disappear again to cooler climes. ... On first reaching Arabia the *hubara* makes for the small new green shoots of grass that come up with the early rains or *wasm* season (October). As the rainy season develops and grass comes up everywhere, the birds scatter and proceed deeper and deeper into the interior, until they are found as far inland in the north as the Syrian desert, and in the south round about Riyadh and the oasis of Jabrin. Except in small numbers, the birds do not penetrate much west of this line.
>
> Round about Zubair, Kuwait and further south as far south as Qatar, the birds are very plentiful throughout the winter, and many thousands of birds are each season killed for food by local Arabs. In Kuwait the Shaikh generally bags about two thousand birds every cold weather, and the combined members of the Al Sa'ud get about the same number in the Najd proper, as also do the Shaikhs of Bahrain, both on their own islands as well as on the mainland where they regularly hunt.

Houbara bustards do still breed in and visit Arabia, albeit in greatly reduced numbers. In earlier times they spread right across the peninsula and were seen all along the northern Tihama on the western coast, as well as in the centre and down the east side. The United Arab Emirates is still a wintering ground for houbara and they are sparsely scattered over their former territories throughout Arabia. Apart from the impact of hunting, they have suffered greatly as a result of habitat deterioration due to goat and sheep grazing in areas previously used as feeding-grounds. However, large areas of the Najd desert have now been taken over by wheat farms, irrigated with fossil water dispersed by central-pivot irrigation systems. It may be that this 'greening of the desert' will bring new opportunities for houbara and indeed for other birds.

The Arabian Gulf has two major flyways for migrating birds: a north-south route through which birds commute between Europe and Pakistan or India, and an east-west route used by birds from Russia passing through Arabia on their way to winter in Africa. Such birds also have to fly over the southern Red Sea in order to reach Africa. Coastal mud-flats, marshes and mangroves of the Arabian Gulf provide important resting places for these migrants and an interesting opportunity for ornithologists to observe some quite rare species. Some birds over-winter in the Gulf itself, returning to northern latitudes as spring approaches. On Bahrain, in January for instance, one may find little egrets, kingfishers and snipe. In mid-February the first signs of spring migration are heralded by the arrival of swallows, house martins, pied wheatears and woodchat shrike, all heading for northern breeding-grounds. During March the spring migration passing over Bahrain gains momentum with flocks of pied wheatear, desert wheatear and common wheatear increasingly numerous. By April the migration is in full swing, the rising volume of bird song announcing arrivals of chiff chaff, willow warbler, redstarts, nightingales, and bee-eaters. By the end of the month it is all over, bar the shouting, until the late summer and early autumn. Wader migration reaches a peak as early as August whilst there is a build-up of passage migrants through September, together with the arrival of winter visitors like common sandpiper. The autumn migration over Bahrain tends to slow in October by which time summer visitors have departed but more and more waders arrive throughout the month and into November, swelling flocks already feeding along the shore.

Migration is imposed upon the lives of many species by climatic cycles. It does not always take place along major horizontal pathways and in south-west Arabia there are several interesting examples of vertically migrating species. Whilst summer conditions in the highlands of the Asir and Yemen mountains provide cool and moist conditions for birds such as the Yemen linnet and Palestine sunbird, in winter these species descend towards the foothills where temperatures are more clement. Rüppell's weaver breeds in the Asir highlands in mid- to late March and then migrates to the Tihama plains below.

Just as Arabian wildlife is temporarily enriched by migrating bird life, it is also augmented by migratory insects, not all of which are welcomed as warmly as the birds! One of the more attractive migratory insects, the painted-lady butterfly (*Vanessa cardui cardui*) is found all over Arabia, even in the Empty Quarter, but its local abundance may fluctuate considerably, subject to migratory patterns and governed by potential and actual breeding grounds. It is a winter resident butterfly in Bahrain for example but does not breed there. On the other hand the painted-lady is a definite breeder in eastern Saudi Arabia, between November and April, producing four broods in this period, before it disappears from the region. At times huge numbers of painted-lady butterflies arrive in parts of Arabia, so numerous that they cannot be ignored. As Torben Larsen, an expert on Arabian butterflies, has pointed out: 'It certainly does not seem able to survive a Lebanese winter or a central Arabian summer, and therefore it has adopted a life-style based on permanent migration, so that part of the total population is always present in any area suitable for breeding.' A mass occurrence of painted-lady butterflies was once reported at Medain Salih, the ancient Nabataean city in Saudi Arabia: larvae in their thousands were feeding on the thistle-herb, *Centaurea,* and large numbers were advancing along with locust nymphs.

Desert locusts depend upon migration for their survival. Occurring in a very broad desert region stretching from the western Sahara to south-west Pakistan, locusts communicate with each other by rubbing their thighs against their wing covers. The penetrating sound acts like a coordinating signal as the flight begins, starting off as small groups, later congregating into dense swarms of migrating locusts. Whilst the desert locust can cause huge damage to crops and potential grazing areas, it has not always been regarded as a pest. To the Assyrians and ancient Egyptians it was a tasty food and biblical references describe it both as a pest and potential sustenance. Locust eggs, laid in the soil, will only hatch in moist conditions and thus random rainfall can greatly influence recruitment. Nymphs, known as hoppers, have undeveloped wings and are unable to fly for several months during which time they feed on local vegetation, sometimes in large armies, with devastating effect. Once they start to fly they are forced to find new sites each day. If numbers are great then the necessity to keep moving is exaggerated by the sheer rate of vegetation consumption by members of the swarm. Locusts have no mechanism for internal temperature regulation so that body temperature fluctuates with that of the immediate environment and flying is restricted mainly to daytime. Each morning, as the sun warms their bodies, they become more lively and eventually take off, wing beats creating a metallic rattle as more and more join the gathering throng. At first the swarm is loosely formed and seems to have no particular direction but by mid-morning the teeming mass becomes more cohesive and rises higher into the air, often climbing to a considerable altitude, borne on thermal air currents. The swarm's flight path generally lies into the wind: locust migrations are very much determined by winds and locusts at the mercy of strong winds are blown passively far from their normal route. There is evidence that they are stimulated in flight by sound and can also orientate with regard to the sun's position.

Prior to the success of locust control programmes, locust plagues were quite common in Arabia, migrating swarms arriving from Ethiopia across the Red Sea, making their first landfall in Yemen. From there the destructive hordes either travelled eastwards, around the southern Arabian coastline, eventually crossing the Arabian Gulf and travelling on through Iran, towards India; or north-east into central Arabia, over the Hijaz, and into the Najd desert or beyond, and into Iraq.

The dramatic effect of one such migration was lucidly described by H. R. P. Dickson, in *The Arab of the Desert*:

> The spring and autumn of 1929 were marked by the number and vastness of the flights of locusts, which ravaged the north-eastern part of Arabia. The autumn rains of that year appeared to have killed off millions of these pests, but they reappeared again in the winter from the direction of Hasa, and in still greater swarms. The female locusts lay their eggs in the warm sand, and it was predicted that the spring of 1930 would see the arrival of the *dibba*, young locusts without wings in the crawling or hopping stage.
>
> Sure enough, in early 1930, Kuwait town suffered from their depredations, and for a few days the inhabitants of Kuwait had, literally, to fight to save anything they had. The date trees of Qusur villages and Jahra were stripped to such an extent that they appeared to have been burnt down by a great conflagration. Indeed one instance was reported of a child deserted by its mother being almost completely eaten by them, though I cannot vouch for the story myself. What finally saved the state on this occasion was a violent southerly storm which blew the hoppers into the Bay of Kuwait.

This was unfortunately not the end of the tale however for shortly afterwards a new plague arrived:

> On 7 April my wife and I visited the area south of the town and found the *dibba* advancing on a four-mile front with a depth of two miles. The ground was seething with them, like a moving and undulating carpet, each *dibba*

marching shoulder to shoulder with its neighbour, and in such a thick mass that as the car drove through them the wheels left regular lanes, as if we were driving through yellow-black snow. The millions of insects which were crushed in this process were instantly devoured by their companions and in a few seconds our car tracks were obliterated. The country through which the insects had passed was stripped quite bare, and where bushes had previously been seen, nothing but bare desert sand remained. Even the thick stalks of large bushes three feet high were entirely devoured.

Such devastation is prevented today by careful control of locusts throughout their range. Without doubt the least welcome migratory species to visit the peninsula, their population has been controlled by Man for the benefit of both himself and a great deal of Arabia's natural wildlife. In our next chapter we see how Man has succeeded in Arabia. We shall be looking at his impact upon Arabian wildlife and his traditional concerns for its wellbeing.

10

Man

in

Arabia

Man has inhabited Arabia for around a million years. As we have seen in previous chapters, both the climate and natural environment were markedly different during the prehistoric phase and sea-levels have fluct-uated to such an extent since then that land bridges linking southern Arabia with Asia and Africa have formed, flooded and then formed again several times. Evidence of Stone Age Man's early presence is scattered across the peninsula in the form of discarded stone tools: hand axes, borers, scrapers, knives and arrow-heads. At some sites the abundance of these archaic artifacts leaves one in no doubt that ancient hunter-gatherers lived here in considerable numbers and were free to wander across much of the peninsula, even into today's hyper-arid deserts such as the Rub al-Khali.

For literally hundreds of thousands of years Stone Age Man hunted the wild game of Arabia, gradually refining techniques for locating, trapping and killing the large animals which roamed across the broad plains and drank from gushing wadis or permanent pools. Over the millennia, and particularly during the last glacial period (70 000 to 10 000 years ago), as climatic shifts altered habitats, many of the larger mammals became extinct. To what extent Man was responsible for this annihilation remains a matter of some conjecture. As an omnivorous species he was unlikely to be in direct competition for food with large herbivorous mammals so long as both lived migratory lives. When Man began to develop farming techniques and settled in one area, however, he would undoubtedly have been forced to protect his grain crops from invading herbivores. As a hunter, Stone Age dwellers of Arabia continued to pursue all mammals actively, both for their meat and their skins.

Given the fact that the chase took place on foot, Man pursuing his quarry armed only with stone-tipped spears or bows and arrows, one is left in admiration of his ingenuity in devising methods to capture the fleet-footed mammals which roamed across the peninsula. Ibex, gazelle, oryx, bubal hartebeeste, wild boar, warthog, hippopotamus, cape hare, leopard, cheetah, caracal, wolf, hyena and bear were all hunted. Many of the herbivores spent spring and summer on higher plateaux where they found rich grazing, returning in the autumn to warmer lowlands. From studies of fossils it is clear that Pleistocene Man had a detailed knowledge and understanding of how herds migrated each spring and autumn between the lowlands and highlands. Families of these Stone Age folk gathered together and settled for a while at vantage points for ambushing game as they filtered through wadis or climbed narrow paths up into fertile escarpments. This method of hunting was almost certainly most effective in spring when hidden archers at many of the sites had the advantage of being down wind from animals scrambling up favourite wadis. In autumn the animals would approach the escarpment edges from a variety of directions, across broad plains, and hunters concealing themselves in the wadis were probably detected by scent.

At other times of year gazelle and oryx were hunted across open country, requiring a different technique, involving the construction of long, v-shaped corrals into which migrating animals were persuaded to wander. Once within the broad entrance of the enormous corral they were quietly encouraged to move towards its apex, becoming increasingly alarmed as they were herded closer and closer together by the converging walls. Finally they had to choose between two options: either to filter through a narrow false exit and become trapped in a high-walled corral, or to jump the high walls in a panicked attempt at escape, breaking limbs in deep pits dug on the far side. Those surmounting this hurdle were brought down by stone-tipped arrows fired by concealed huntsmen.

173

We can only guess at the enormous efforts made by these ancient nimrods, or at their successes in killing large numbers of quarry. Remains of these ancient traps, known as desert kites, are still found in parts of the peninsula, and numerous stone arrow-heads are found around their outer walls. The traps seem to have been so successful that they were never completely abandoned by Man, but were re-used year after year, with additions or repairs to their walls being carried out over a very long period. Indeed, some of the desert kites have survived into present times and we have several written accounts of their use in capturing gazelle during the first half of this century. One such account, written by Aharoni in 1946, is particularly graphic. The translated version not only provides a unique insight into the Bedouin use of these ancient traps but also illustrates the huge numbers of gazelle which recently inhabited Arabia.

Once I made a four-day excursion into the desert with Baron von Wirtenau in order to observe the migration of gazelles. We observed them with binoculars and saw innumerable flocks, one after the other. Our estimate was that we saw more than 10 000, all of which were returning from north to south. They start their migrations in herds of thousands, and the Bedouin know this time well and hunt them during the migration.

I and Y. Hankin, my hunter and reliable companion in desert travels, witnessed once a shocking spectacle, when 500–600 gazelle were trapped in a corral not far from Racheimah. The length of the corral which we saw was several kilometres and there were many of them in the desert. I asked several Bedouin we met when these structures were erected and all of them gave the same answer: 'In old times. The fathers of the fathers of our fathers already found them here.'

In order to trap several hundred gazelle at once, the Bedouin enclose a large triangular area which extends over many kilometres. In the wall, which is higher than a man, are places which are lower, and before each one a deep trench is dug. . . . The gazelles were not afraid, as the walls, built from desert stone, were similar to their surrounding. When several hundred gazelle had entered the corral, the Bedouin closed in on them, running from left to right, shouting ferociously. Then the frightened gazelle tried to escape, jumping over the walls at the lower parts of it, and fell into the trenches outside of them. We saw how many of them were pulled out of the trenches with broken limbs and their bleeting in agony was heart rending. The Bedouin however were not impressed by the suffering of their victims and cut their throats before they died. Then they loaded the gazelles onto their camels, brought them to their camp, skinned them and salted the meat.

Around 15 000 years ago, towards the end of the last ice age, Arabia began to dry. Its permanent pools shrank and wadis no longer carried permanent rivers or streams. Now it became necessary for the inhabitants to follow natural migrations of wildlife, moving with the seasons and influenced by random patterns of rainfall. The deserts became increasingly arid and more and more difficult for Man to inhabit or even to traverse. Increasingly human settlements were concentrated around the coastline of the peninsula, where food could always be found in the form of shellfish, fish or even large sea-cows, and where contacts with other communities could be established and maintained through maritime trading.

The oldest Arabian house is in Qatar and is around 7000 years old (5020 BC). It comprised a small hut made from sandstone built close to the shores of the Arabian Gulf. Most dwellings were made from reeds, mud and palm-fronds and it is therefore unsurprising that they have not been preserved. The first semi-permanent settlements on Bahrain have been dated to around 6000 years ago. They are marked by shell middens; huge piles

174

of discarded marine molluscan shells (suitable for radio-carbon dating) and the remains of 6000-year-old meals. From such finds we know that fishermen at this time were using shallow fish-traps and were curing their catches. Different levels in the shell middens reflect the development of fishing techniques: boats were used in later years and deeper water fish, or even dugongs, added to the seasonal harvests.

Gradually these settlements provided the basis for new civilizations such as Dilmun, along the Gulf shores of the Arabian peninsula and on its off-lying islands (eastern Saudi Arabia and Bahrain), or Magan, in the area which is now the United Arab Emirates and Oman. As the great Sumerian civilization, rooted in the valley of the Tigris and Euphrates close to the head of the Gulf, burgeoned in importance and its trading vessels plied the seas, Dilmun and Magan also expanded, reaching their zenith, around 4000 years ago. Our knowledge of the links between Sumeria, Dilmun and Magan are based upon finds of pottery fragments, ancient insignia seals, bronze figurines, other artifacts and even written accounts on clay tablets, the oldest historical records in existence.

Excavations in eastern Saudi Arabia, near Dhahran, and on Bahrain have revealed to us the extent and importance of the Dilmunite civilization as well as some interesting insights into the lives of its people. We have learned, for example, that pearl-diving was practised in the Arabian Gulf at least 4300 years ago. The oldest known gold and pearl-earring has been found in a 5000-year-old grave on Bahrain and a midden of pearl-shells was unearthed in which fragments of 'Barbar-ware' pottery point to its association with the height of Dilmun's development. At least 172 000 burial mounds are located on Bahrain, of which 150 000 are from the Early Bronze Age (4800 to 3800 BP), a clear indication of the importance of this ancient Arabian civilization.

The first signs of civilization in southern Arabia are grave mounds built just over 5000 years ago, containing Mesopotamian-type pottery. The community, architects of these graves, located in what is today the United Arab Emirates, became an important half-way trading-post linking the contemporary river valley civilizations of Meluhha in Pakistan, and Meso-potamia in Iraq. Graves at Umm al Nar, on the island of Abu Dhabi, have revealed indications of this trade, including a 4600-year-old pot decorated with the hump-backed bull of Kulli in Baluchistan. Excavations on houses at Umm al Nar unearthed shark's tooth amulets and copious remains of sea-cows or dugongs which formed an important part of the inhabitants' diet.

It also seems likely that copper mined from the hills of Oman was transported down to these shores before being shipped to the head of the

175

Gulf, via Dilmun (Bahrain). The concept is an intriguing one since it suggests both the stimulus for, and the timing of, the earliest domestication of the camel. We know that the camel was naturally present in southern Arabia at this time (around 5000 years ago) because tomb slabs at Umm al Nar were engraved with camels and their bones were excavated from the stone houses of the settlement. Camel bones were even carved into domestic implements such as spindle whorls. Of course, this is not proof that the camel was already a domestic animal, but if it was not, then one is left with the question of how the inhabitants of Umm al Nar managed to carry copper all the way from the Hajar mountains of present-day Oman. It is known that considerable quantities of copper were taken out of Magan. In one case a shipment received at Dilmun weighed 18.5 metric tons, paid for in Dilmun by wool, garments, skins and sesame oil. The route down from the mountains and all the way to the coastal island of Abu Dhabi involves a 150-kilometre trek across desert from the oasis of Al Ain. It must have been a daunting journey in those days and virtually impossible with a large weight of copper. It seems highly likely that camels were brought into service as beasts of burden at this time, the first place in the world where this occurred.

176 Although the civilization of Magan waned and the culture of Umm al Nar disappeared around 4000 years ago, its people took with them, wherever it was they travelled to, a secret which was to open the door to a new phase in Man's settlement of Arabia. It was also at this time that desertification accelerated and much of Arabia became virtually uninhabitable. The people of southern Arabia, having domesticated the camel, were beginning to use it as a means of crossing the great stretches of desert which had previously hindered their progress. Apart from transport the camel provided milk, meat and the material for camel's hair tents.

Domestication of the camel brought with it the need to obtain regular grazing for their animals. In a region of low and sporadic rainfall the only solution was to keep moving to new pastures, wherever rain had fallen in recent months. And so was born the tradition of nomadism which has characterized much of Arabian life right up to the present day. As Saad Abdullah Sowayan comments in his erudite study, *Nabati Poetry: The Oral Poetry of Saudi Arabia*: 'Nomadism in Arabia is both necessitated and facilitated by the camel'.

For some people, however, the urge to maintain a permanent base became paramount. The problem was how to control the availability of fresh water. A key came in the development of underground water channels, part of a sophisticated method of irrigation known as the *falaj* system. This provided a means of carrying water across a considerable distance of semi-desert to

The high valleys and mountains of Wadi Dahr and the Hajja region in the Yemen (previous page and left) have been terraced and irrigated for thousands of years. Always the most populated region of Arabia, it was described by the ancient Greek writer Agatharchides of Cnidus in the second century BC: '... Sabaeans who are the most populous of the Arabian peoples. They inhabit the region called Eudaemon Arabia (Fortunate Arabia) which bears most of the products considered valuable by us. It also supports herds of animals of all kinds in untold abundance. A natural sweet smell pervades the whole country because almost all plants which are pre-eminent for their fragrance grow unceasingly.... In the interior there are dense forests in which there are large frankincense and myrrh trees and in addition palm trees, calamus, and cinnamon trees and others which have a fragrance similar to these.'

179

Nature's bounty has not always been benevolent. Apart from cyclical swarms of locusts, scorpions (top left) and camel spiders (below left), both of which can grow to more than 10 centimetres, have caused devastation in the past. Agatharchides reported one such incident: 'The region adjacent to the Locust-Eaters is large and has pasturage that is exceptional in its variety but is completely deserted and inaccessible to all the peoples who live nearby. It did not originally thus lack human inhabitants but became so because of unbelievable swarms of scorpions and spiders which some call "Four-Jaws". For people say that this species grew greatly in numbers after a heavy rain; and the inhabitants, who were unable to endure this plague, chose salvation by flight over their homeland and left that territory empty of people.' The picture far left shows the deserted village of Yanbu al Nakl.

Large areas of central Arabia are now being irrigated from vast underground water reservoirs. Drilling techniques developed for oil extraction are employed and a watering system known as central-pivot irrigation (above), is used to spray water onto thousands of circular green wheat fields. The new water sources and the associated botanical and insect life have become magnets for bird life. The number of bird species found in central Arabia has trebled in the last 10 years.

The transportability of water and the ready availability of fodder has brought prosperity and security to the Bedouin in recent years. Livestock populations have increased dramatically and large numbers of sheep and goats are transported to regions where the sparse natural vegetation rapidly becomes over-grazed (right). The preservation of rangeland and the restoration of botanical diversity is the principal focus for Arabian conservation organizations.

Four-wheel drive vehicles (above) long ago replaced the camel as the mode of desert transport and have made all parts of the desert accessible, not only to the Bedouin but to hunting parties from the towns. The extinction of the Arabian ostrich, the near extinction of the Arabian oryx and gazelle species, together with the great decline in the number of bustard, are all directly attributable to the ease with which it has become possible to pursue game.

Harrat al Harrah Wildlife Reserve in north-west Saudi Arabia covers an area of 17 000 square kilometres and is a vast, treeless laval plain (above).

Temminck's horned lark is one of seven members of the lark family to breed here (below right). The area contains the largest concentrations of breeding larks in the entire Palaearctic region. Many migrating desert birds like the houbara bustard will only settle and breed if sufficient spring growth appears.

It is bitterly cold in winter and searingly hot in summer. The brief spring lasts only a few weeks but during the five years since the reserve has been protected from sheep and goats, spring flowering and associated insect life have brought a great increase in wildlife activity (left).

The Arabian oryx (left) is highly adapted to desert life and can withstand great heat. Its acute sense of smell enables it to locate remote areas of desert vegetation. Oryx have been known to walk 80 kilometres in a single night, can eat most desert plants and survive the summer by digging out plant roots. The Arabian oryx was saved from extinction by an elaborate international conservation effort. The present world population is close to 1000 and it has been successfully re-introduced into the wild in both Oman and Saudi Arabia. Like the oryx, desert gazelle such as the rheem (above) extract all the water they need from plants. However, gazelle numbers have also greatly declined due to hunting and displacement. The Saudi gazelle has recently become extinct in the wild and the five other species are in danger of a similar fate.

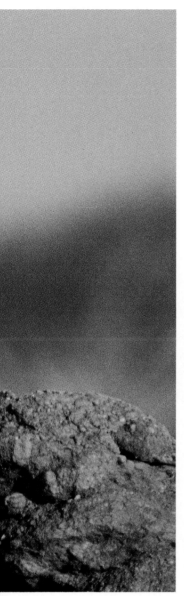

Both the red fox and the endangered desert sand cat (left and below) live in caves or deep burrows and are active at night. The sand cat is so well adapted to desert life that the soles of its feet are entirely covered with hairs which enable it to walk rapidly over soft sand without sinking. Both creatures regulate their body temperatures by panting and are also able to dissipate heat through their large ears. This lowers body temperature without loss of body liquid. They feed on a mixed diet of insects and lizards.

Every year some 2000 to 3000 million birds migrate through Arabia to Europe, Asia and Africa. The Red Sea coastline is an important migratory pathway, lesser crested terns (left) are one of six species to breed on the Farasan Islands in south-western Saudi Arabia.

Steppe eagles (above) migrate on a broad front moving back and forth between the summer breeding grounds in the U.S.S.R and their wintering ground in Africa. They depend upon the rising air of the thermals to gain elevation and in late September 40 000 steppe eagles a day cross from Arabia to Africa by the narrow strait of Bab al Mandeb. The blue-cheeked bee-eater (overleaf) is a summer and autumn visitor nesting colonially in holes in sandy banks.

a village or farm. A series of vertical well shafts were dug, starting perhaps at the base of a mountain or in a wadi and then at regular intervals, as far as the main delivery point. These shafts were connected towards their bases by horizontal tunnels, creating a long underground conduit. It was a system which was to have as much influence on settled life in Arabia as did the camel for its nomadic inhabitants.

The use of camels as pack-animals had another vital influence upon Arabian life and on the whole future pattern of settlement on the peninsula. Transportation of goods by camel-train began to replace sea transport and fixed routes became firmly estabished for passage through Arabia, from its southern shores to its northern boundaries. The two great advantages of these camel-trains over sea transport was that, firstly, one was no longer at the mercy of northerly winds which blow for much of the year in the Red Sea and Gulf and, secondly, loss of goods due to shipwrecks or piracy was no longer a danger. Camel herdsmen of southern Arabia amassed fortunes from transporting goods, originating in India or Africa, from southern Arabian ports such as Aden, to Egypt and the Mediterranean world to the north. The ancient world's insatiable desire for perfumes and incense was met by frankincense and other plants from southern Arabia which were also carried to the northern markets on camels. The commercial success of camel-traders, and the need to protect oases or wells for their own use, fostered inter-family rivalries and the advent of local warfare.

The mountains of Yemen and south-west Saudi Arabia, in addition to providing a source of aromatic plants, also yielded other valuable commodities including that most sought after metal: gold. This rich, well-watered land developed its own culture; the Saba or Sheba mentioned in the Bible, later to be known as 'Arabia Felix'. There were basically three caravan trails by which the desirable wares of south Arabia, India and Africa were ferried northwards: one up the east coast, one along the west coast, and a third tracking from west to east through central Arabia. Along their routes small cities, dependent on oases or spring-fed wadis, expanded into cosmopolitan centres of international trade. One such city in Saudi Arabia now lies partially buried beneath desert sands: Taima was at the height of its importance 3000 years ago. Indeed, the neo-Babylonian king Nabonidus moved to the city, protected by a seven-mile surrounding wall, and built his palace there. Saudi Arabian archaeologists have found a fascinating inscribed stone in a cult temple there which combines religious symbols from Babylonia, Egypt and Mesopotamia.

Another major caravan city in southern Saudi Arabia was Najran, situated close to the Yemen border: an enchanting walled and towered city with a turbulent past, whose key location at the bifurcation of westerly and easterly

193

caravan routes greatly enhanced its commercial and strategic significance. One hundred and seventy-six kilometres north of Najran, on the same caravan route, is the ancient city of Qarayat al Fau which flourished between 2000 and 3000 years ago. Deserted, buried, lost, and forgotten for centuries, it was rediscovered by ARAMCO staff in the 1940s. Subsequently it has been extensively excavated under the direction of Professor Abdul Rahman al Ansary of the University of Riyadh, who has used it for teaching purposes. Discoveries at al Fau have re-emphasized the great wealth generated by caravan routes and the international flavour of its staging-posts. As time passed, and camel-train profits continued to amass, some cities became truly magnificent, their grandeur preserved as a result of a unique construction method perfected by the Nabateans who carved many edifices out of sheer, pink-tinged, sandstone cliff-faces.

Petra in Jordan and Medain Saleh in Saudi Arabia are living monuments to this creativity and ingenuity. Both cities owed their existence to the commerce created by the caravan routes, in turn a product of domestication of the camel. The first westerner to visit the fabulous remains of Medain Saleh was Jean Louis Burckhardt in 1812. Medain Saleh's pre-eminence lay in its position at the convergence of two major arms of the camel-train routes: to the north lay Petra from which branches led to Egypt, Jerusalem and Syria; to the north-east the route from Medain Saleh wound through Taima to Al Jauf where it branched again, continuing north-eastwards to Babylon or tracking off to the north-west, towards Syria and south toward Najran and Dhofar.

The Greek Empire extended its influence to northern Arabia: confirmed by Hellenistic remains at several sites on the peninsula, notably the Kuwaiti island of Failaka in the Arabian Gulf, supposedly a base for Alexander's fleet under its Admiral, Nearchus. The remains of a Greek temple have been excavated on the island. On the mainland, the caravan city of Thaj, in north-eastern Saudi Arabia and one of the largest ancient cities in the Kingdom, has also been investigated. Finds from there, including Hellenistic pottery, confirm that this walled and fortified inland city traded with parts of the Greek Empire. These ancient links are illustrated in the following quote as is the importance of the camel to the people there:

> The land bordering the mountainous area is inhabited by Arabs who are called Debae. They are camel raisers who rely on this beast for all the most important necessities of life. They fight against their enemies from these animals, and they easily accomplish all their business by transporting their wares loaded on their backs. They lived by drinking their milk, and they roam their whole country on racing camels. A river runs through the middle of their country which carries down so many nuggets of gold that the silt

which is deposited at its mouths gleams. The natives are completely without experience in the working of gold, but they are hospitable to strangers, not to all visitors, however, but only to those from Boeotia and the Peloponnesus because of some ancient bond of kinship derived from Heracles with this people, which they say has been handed down in mythical form from their ancestors.

On the Erythraean Sea, Agatharchides of Cnidus
(second century BC)

In Roman times south-west Arabia was known as 'Arabia Felix' or fortunate Arabia. Wadi Hadramaut in the south was the centre of a great spice trade: aromatic frankincense was much in demand from the Dhofar region where it is still collected in the traditional manner today, from trees of *Boswellia*. To the Romans, control of the trading routes with southern Arabia justified a military mission backed up by infra-structural developments. Thus, following Pompey's victories over Syria-Palestine in 64–63 BC, the Romans consolidated their grip on northern Arabia, focusing on the region east of the Dead Sea, known then as Peraea, and today occupied by Jordan. The southern kingdom of Nabataea held on to its independence however until AD 106 when Trajan's forces finally reached a rapprochement with the inhabitants of Petra, allowing them to gain control. Five years later the Romans pushed their road link through to Aqaba, completing a new route for chariots from the northern Syrian city of Bosra to the shores of the Gulf of Aqaba, linked to the Red Sea. As the Romans moved south, towards central Arabia, they built forts and sallied forth from these in vain attempts to control Safaitic and Thamudic desert tribes who were far better adapted to life in this harsh landscape.

Archaeological records of these desert people are found in numerous rock engravings all over Arabia. Among the narrow crevices in sheer cliffs forming the buttress-like walls of Wadi Rum in southern Jordan one finds unique inscriptions chiselled by independent camel-traders. A survey of all rock art sites in Saudi Arabia, organized by the Department of Antiquities and Museums, has revealed the great wealth of culture among the peninsula's desert-dwellers. Between 1984 and 1987 studies of rock art in northern Saudi Arabia, particularly between Tabuk and Haql, along the ancient caravan route, revealed 311 sites with over 7000 individual carvings, including many representations of people, animals, plants, tools and Kufic or Thamudic writing. The art has been classified into four basic periods of the desert's occupation: an early hunter-gatherer phase, an intermediate phase, a literate phase and finally inscriptions from the Islamic era. Carved in stone, the story of Arabia is poignantly revealed by this rock art.

On a rock face at Jubbah, near the boundary of the Nafud desert,

195

85 kilometres north of the Saudi Arabian city of Hail, there are carvings attributed to the early period comprising life-size representations of tall thin men, some over 2 metres high, wearing flat head-dresses, belts with elongated tassels, and often carrying hunting tools. Many of the animals are bovine, characteristically piebald with long horns. They were clearly the predominant domestic animals of this early period, around 12 000 years ago. Similar carvings occur elsewhere in Arabia, at Taif, Abha, Obhur north of Jeddah, Bir Hima, Jebel Qara, Jebel Kaukab and Jebel Mulkan on the road between Jeddah and Taif.

Rocks at wadis Dum, Baqar and Asafir in the vicinity of Tabuk in northern Arabia and also in south-west parts of the peninsula, at *jebels* Qara and Kaukab, display art associated with the intermediate phase (8000 BP to 4000 BP) characterized by illustrations of domestic cattle, sheep, goats, and, in the latter period, camels. Scenes of hunting are depicted, together with pastoral activities indicating that farming was becoming established. The advent of writing in Arabia is reflected by a literate phase in its rock art: Graphic carvings now intermingle with signs, figures depicting scenes of hunting or pastoralism with inscriptions in one or more of the semitic languages, dating back to the first millennium BC.

196

Increasingly, after 1800 BP, desiccation of Arabia, allied with decline of great northern empires which had provided important markets for its products, extracted a heavy toll on life in the peninsula. Ancient trade routes generated a great dispersion of Arabian families throughout the region and helped to establish Bedouin tribes as true masters of their immense desert domain. Whilst many of the ancient cities of Arabia, influenced by regional conflicts, trade depressions or climatic changes, entered a period of general decline, the people of the desert remained strongly independent, maintaining their traditional life-style as a source of enduring strength and stability in an ever changing world.

Approximately 1800 years ago many of the inhabitants of Yemen, belonging at that time to a tribal group known as the Azdites, moved north-eastwards onto the west and south-west slopes of the Hajar mountains, leaving the eastern slopes of Jebel al Akhdar to tribes who owed their allegiance to the Persians. Persian influence in Arabia continued to make itself felt until the Prophet Muhammad galvanized and united the major families of the peninsula in a uniquely successful pan-Arab mission. The message of Islam spread across Arabia replacing a variety of sun- and fire-worshipping cults with a faith which provided spiritual unity and imparted a strong sense of purpose.

From that point forward the story of Man in Arabia is inextricably linked with the rise of Islam as the religion of the peninsula and as the guiding force in the lives of its people. From a historical perspective the new era became known as the Islamic Period. As in the preceding millennia, two cultures continued to live side by side in Arabia: settled people living in villages and towns, existing on agriculture or commerce, and nomadic Bedouin who regularly moved across the peninsula, herding camels, goats or sheep. The Bedouin, during more than 4000 years of desert life, had become truly skilled in the art of survival in this wilderness landscape.

The term 'arab' was used by both Greeks and Babylonians to describe the desert inhabitants of the peninsula. The Bedouin still refer to themselves as *a'rab*. The term Europeans use, *bedouin*, is derived from the town-dweller's description, based on the Arabic: *badawi* (singular) or *badu* (plural), meaning 'desert-dweller'. Bedouin life is ruled by the tenets of Islam and by their environment. Tribal membership is established through the male line and historically large tribes used to control territories. The home of the Bedouin is the desert. His traditional house was a tent of simple construction, ideally suited for desert life. Made from camel hair woven by women of the family, the *bait al-sha'ar* (house of hair) was easily erected or rolled up and carried on the back of a camel. Walls of the tent could be lifted in daytime to improve ventilation, or dropped to provide privacy or warmth.

A Bedouin man would move into his own tent after his marriage. Since the construction was flexible, he would have started off with a single-poled tent and graduated, over the years, to larger two- or three-poled structures as his children were born and his needs increased. A Bedouin tent is still arranged so that the two basic spheres of Bedouin traditional life can be accommodated: it has an area, open to the front flaps, where men meet and the owner offers hospitality to his male guests, and a side portion, closed from public view, in which the whole family sleep and where the wife cooks, cares for the children, and entertains her own friends.

197

A key symbol of Bedouin, and indeed of Arabic hospitality is the serving of tea and coffee. The fire where this is brewed is generally on the floor in the centre of the men's front tent section (*al-shigg*). A visitor is first offered tea brewed by his host in a kettle resting on the fire and poured from there into a small glass already containing a large amount of white sugar. After this, coffee is either poured from an already simmering pot or is freshly brewed. It is a familiar ritual followed in every Bedouin tent and has been transferred to the settled community so that today's visitor to a commercial office will be offered the same sequence of drinks, served in the same way, signifying the same welcome.

Bedouin traditions pervade every aspect of their existence, providing solid foundations for a well-balanced life. Their deep understanding of the desert and unique insight into its ecology dictate conservation methods which pre-date any efforts made in modern times. Use of falcons in hunting houbara and hare did not cause permanent damage to any of the wildlife populations involved so long as Bedouin travelled by camel or on horse-back. Their grazing animals did not make any significant impact on desert vegetation until trucks were used to bring large numbers of sheep to remote desert sites watered by diesel-driven pumps. Bedouin livestock existed in balance with large herds of gazelle and oryx. Under a system called *hima* land was preserved for long-term benefit of the tribe, rather than short-term gain, and has become a model for today's conservationists. Under the *hima* system rangeland was set aside for times of drought and for the use of armies on the move. Only in times of great difficulty were people allowed to cut fodder from the protected *hima* area and even then only by hand. Animals were seldom allowed to graze in the *hima*. It is for this reason that the ancient *himas* are of great interest to modern-day botanists who are finding unique Arabian plant types no longer existing in the surrounding regions.

Predating Islam, the Arabian *hima* grazing system is possibly the oldest effective method of rangeland conservation to be found worldwide. A remarkable aspect of this conservation method is that it evolved in Arabia's deserts where pastures were always in short supply and where tremendous discipline was involved in leaving a particular area of rangeland untouched. The *hima* system received the support of the Prophet Muhammad who realized that the strength of the Islamic nation depended upon its ability to provide adequate grazing for livestock and armies on the move. Therefore he set aside areas to be used as special reserves, protecting them from everyday grazing and allowing vegetation to become firmly established.

Over the course of time, five different types of *hima* became established, comprising areas where: (a) animal grazing is prohibited but where grass may be cut during droughts, under strict control of the tribal leader; (b) grazing and/or cutting is permitted but only at certain times of year; (c) grazing is permitted throughout the year but the kind and number of grazing animals is strictly controlled; (d) the reserve is maintained for bees and grazing is prohibited or strictly controlled during the following season; and finally, (e) the reserve is established for protection of forest trees such as juniper, acacia or the salt-bush *ghada* (*Haloxylon persicum*). Recent studies on this ancient practice of land management have shown that it is highly efficient and that grazing lands have been maintained for long periods in balance with livestock.

In places the effect of *hima* protection is really dramatic. For example, 80 kilometres north of Riyadh, *Hima Hureimla* has long been maintained in an area of extremely low rainfall (less than 80 millimetres per year). The *hima* is along part of a wadi where grazing is strictly controlled. Comparisons of vegetation, both upstream and downstream of the protected area, with that inside the *hima* leaves one in absolutely no doubt regarding its efficacy. Twenty-eight thousand *Acacia* were counted in a square kilometre area of the *hima* whilst not a single *Acacia* tree was found on either side, along the same wadi, either upstream or downstream. Even a water-retaining dyke outside the *hima* had failed to stimuate much vegetation compared to that covering the ground in the area protected from grazing. There are many other examples of this system and the method is still used in Saudi Arabia where, at the latest count, over 3000 *hima* are still in existence.

The history of Man's presence in Arabia has been one of both struggle against and adaptation to the natural environment. The balance between Man and the natural world, carefully nurtured for thousands of years, has been much changed during the present century by the impact of modernity. We examine just how this has happened in the next chapter.

199

Modernity
and
Change

In the early part of this century the Arabian Gulf countries were largely dependent upon income from pearl fishing, the export of dates and animal skins, trading gold and the re-export of various goods carried on dhows from Africa and India.

The pearling industry has played a central role in Gulf life since Babylonian times. In the early 1900s over 20 000 men from Bahrain alone were engaged in the seasonal pursuit of natural pearls. Despite the great hardship and danger suffered by the pearl divers, it was the main source of employment and income for entire communities.

The sight of hundreds of dhows heading off to the pearling banks could not fail to move any observer left on shore. Charles Belgrave, a political advisor in Bahrain during the 1930s, recalled his first impression of such an experience:

> I shall never forget the first time I saw the pearling fleet heading out from Muharraq. It was evening and the tide was full. The graceful ships like Roman galleys with huge lateen sails moved smoothly through the iridescent water, silhouetted against the sunset sky. The sound of sailors singing and the throbbing of their drums was borne across the water to where I stood with the people who were watching the departure.

He was one of the last Europeans to witness such scenes for the pearling industry was rapidly coming to an end as Japanese cultured pearls came on the market in the 1930s.

Arabia's oil industry was initiated in 1925 with the granting of the first exploration concession. The first well near Jebel ad Dukhan in Bahrain, which started delivering 9600 barrels a day in 1932, is preserved as a historic monument to the birth of a new era not just for Bahrain but for the whole of Arabia.

200

However, it was not until the 1950s that sufficient wealth was generated by oil sales to alter radically the traditional ways of life. When that change did come it came with astonishing speed and transformed the face of the entire peninsula. Even the economies of countries without oil, like the Yemen, were profoundly changed as two million Yemenis left to work in the oil-rich countries of the Gulf.

Today, roads link the most remote parts of Arabia. Most people have access to hospitals, education, a high standard of living and social security much like and often better than that found in European countries. Along the edge of the Arabian Gulf, new cities, recreational and industrial projects now occupy hundreds of miles of coastline and most people live in modern cities built upon western models.

Agricultural projects fed by immense quantities of aquifer water have turned large areas of the desert green and engineering projects have dammed water. Desalination plants and air-conditioning provide a ready supply of water to coastal cities and air-conditioning helps to create a productive working environment even when temperatures outside reach 50° Centigrade. Fodder and grain subsidies, four-wheel drive vehicles and water-tankers have brought security and prosperity to the Bedouin and herds of sheep, goats and camels have multiplied.

However, a feature of rapidly developing countries is that social changes have come well ahead of administrative and legislative dictates. The Arabian countries have been no exception to this rule and much development has taken place without adequate regard for long-term environmental impact.

Coastal developments along the Arabian Gulf have often involved extensive land reclamation of intertidal beaches, mangrove bays and sea-grass beds. These places are the productive hatcheries for much marine life. In Tarat Bay, the largest sea-grass bed, 40 per cent of the sea-grasses have disappeared.

Locust control, eradication of malaria and modern agriculture have been the justification for the widespread use of insecticides which have killed off many potentially useful insects, animals, birds and even reptiles. Entire ecosystems have been affected since many of the flowering plants depend upon pollination by insects and many animals have been deprived of their main food resource.

Two of the first signs of the modern era in the Arabian interior were the introduction of the Enfield rifle and, somewhat later, the motor car. To the Bedouin the rifle was a real improvement and when used to hunt game for family needs, did not have a major impact on wildlife. The more accurate gun improved their chances of making a clean kill rather than injuring a gazelle which may have escaped to suffer and perhaps to die days later.

Combined with the motor car, however, it was a different story. The motor car and, more recently, the four-wheel drive vehicle brought people from the towns into the desert; people who had not lived the nomadic life of the Bedouin and who did not depend upon wildlife for food, but simply killed for sport. It was the beginning of the end for Arabia's gazelle, oryx and ibex. The gazelle of the open, stone plains where cars could roam freely, were the first to disappear.

Wilfred Thesiger is probably the greatest chronicler of desert travel and also the last European to have crossed the Rub al-Khali by camel. Like many admirers of the great resourcefulness of the Bedouin, he laments the implications of modern change:

> I went to southern Arabia only just in time. Others will go there to study geology and archaeology, the birds and plants and animals, even to study the Arabs themselves, but they will move about in cars and keep in touch with the outside world by wireless. They will bring back results far more interesting than mine but they will never know the spirit of the land or the greatness of the Arabs.
>
> *Arabian Sands, 1959*

In the pre-oil era, both wildlife and Man were severely constrained by the natural availability of fresh water. Drilling technology, introduced to the peninsula for the extraction of oil, also led to the discovery of large, underground freshwater reservoirs: the residue of Arabia's pluvial period many thousands of years ago. Modern pumping and piping systems were employed to extract huge quantities of water for farms, villages and cities. For a time it seemed as if there were no constraints on how much water the gigantic, underground reservoirs could supply but all too soon, the effects of extraction became apparent as the water-tables fell significantly.

Intensive crop irrigation based mainly on central-pivot irrigation systems took Saudi Arabia's wheat production from 160 000 tons per year in 1975 to 3.3 million tons a year in 1988. The water which fuelled much of this impressive agricultural development is drawn from depths of 1000 metres or more. In transforming huge areas of unproductive land into high yielding wheat fields, it also brought about dramatic changes to the natural wildlife in areas under development and these new green oases have become a beacon for birdlife. It is estimated that between two and three thousand million birds migrate across Arabia each year.

Along the Arabian Gulf coast massive desalination plants supply the drinking water and domestic needs of entire cities. Industrial projects are also using sea-water both as a source of fresh water and for cooling purposes. The effects of this intensive use of coastal sea-water on shallow marine habitats is still under investigation. Both coral reefs and sea-grass beds are at risk and the long-term consequences remain unknown.

The increasing availability of fresh water to burgeoning towns and cities has brought with it another problem: how to handle waste water. Whereas in most parts of the world waste water is channelled back to the sea, either directly or via rivers, in Arabia treated waste water is used for urban irrigation, creating parks and verdant road verges; or it is piped into the desert where it forms artificial rivers and new wetlands. The impact of this waste water irrigation on the appearance of Arabian towns and the ecologies of surrounding deserts has been impressive. Travellers who visited Arabian cities twenty years ago would hardly recognize them today. Places like Jeddah, Riyadh, Manama, Kuwait City, Abu Dhabi and Dubai are so green in parts that it is hard to believe that these are desert cities where previously the only greenery to be seen was in the confined spaces of sparingly watered gardens. The improvements are not only of benefit to Man since the increased greenery has had a marked effect on other animals, especially birds.

Saudi Arabia's capital city, Riyadh, now has over 60 municipal parks, numerous tree-lined boulevards and a superabundance of private gardens (many containing swimming-pools) literally brimming with cultivated grass, flowers, bushes and trees. The scene for an over-flying bird, *en route* from Eurasia to Africa, has become increasingly tempting over the past decade. Many have succumbed and over-winter in the heart of Arabia, rather than continuing further south. The city's bird population has shown a significant increase in numbers of various species, especially ring-necked parakeets, collared doves and other urban adapted birds, but the really dramatic change is to be found at the Al Hair reserve south of Riyadh where treated sewage water has created a new wetland, 30 miles long, in total contrast with the surrounding desert. This reserve is so attractive to resident and migrant birds that the number of species sighted at Al Hair has gone up from 90 to 270 in ten years.

Dense reed-beds, tamarisk clumps, gravel banks and shallow pools watered by the city's effluent provide an attractive environment for a wide variety of birds including many water-associated species such as the moorhen (*Gallinula chloropus*) and mallard (*Anas platyrhynchos*). Over 100 breeding pairs of black-winged stilt (*Himantopus himantopus*) are well established there now whilst the avocet (*Recurvirostra avosetta*) has also begun breeding. A recent check-list from the region listed 278 species, the majority of which owe their presence to the newly formed wetland.

Whilst other similar examples of wetland creation occur throughout Arabia there are also many cases where natural wetland habitats have

203

been cleared, drained, filled in and built upon, totally destroying natural environments of key importance to wildlife. Surface water sources, such as the Azraq oasis in Jordan, and the Leyla Lakes in central Arabia have been reduced in size through increased extraction of fresh water, causing pressures on natural vegetation and bird life. Coastal wetlands primarily comprised mangrove thickets which once fringed large sectors of the Arabian Gulf shoreline. The mangroves created their own richly productive environment of great importance to many juvenile marine fish and crustaceans. Virtually all of the mangroves on the coast of the Arabian Gulf have been destroyed, and large areas of the intertidal zone have unfortunately been filled as part of land-reclamation projects with apparent disregard for the vital role it plays in the overall ecology of coastal environments. Fish and shrimp nursery grounds have been greatly reduced.

Parts of the Gulf have not fared much better. Many shallow-water corals and sea-grasses have been killed by clouds of fine silt disturbed by dredging operations. In turn, the destruction of shallow-water sea-grass beds has had a considerable impact on shrimps, fish, turtles and dugongs. Sea turtles require shallow productive feeding grounds and undisturbed nesting beaches. Their numbers are being depleted through reduction of these important habitats. Dugongs depend upon extensive sea-grass beds. Across the entire Indo-Pacific their numbers have been decreasing towards extinction levels. Arabia's threatened population may represent one of the last potentially viable breeding stocks of this placid marine mammal. Pollution from industrial projects has combined with oil pollution and sewage to cause an over-all deterioration in water quality. Intensive fishing, spear-fishing, coral-collecting and shell-collecting by expatriates and local people has damaged the more accessible reefs whilst over-fishing has affected commercial stocks.

Damage to rangelands has resulted from improved access in the form of an extensive new road network and widespread abandonment of the traditional land-use plans administered by local tribes. Headage subsidies and high prices have promoted increased stocking with consequent over-grazing and extensive damage to natural vegetation. Confirmation of this is graphically presented at the fenced boundaries of wildlife reserves such as Shaumeri in Jordan or Al Areen in Bahrain. In both cases grasses and shrubs inside the fence (where small numbers of wild animals are kept) are tall and luxuriant, whilst outside the ground is almost bare. The contrast is entirely due to the presence outside and absence inside of grazing sheep and goats. In some areas sheep, which could never have reached desert-grazing areas on foot, are transported by pick-ups or trucks and ground water is pumped to the surface in order to augment rainfall irrigation. Both the water-table and natural vegetation are severely affected by this practice and wildlife is effectively excluded from regions which ought to be available to them for natural grazing.

Two Saudi Arabian organizations deeply committed to tackling the problem of rangeland deterioration through over-grazing by domestic animals are the Meteorology and Environmental Protection Administration and the National Commission for Wildlife Conservation and Development. A recent report on the situation in Saudi Arabia called for urgent government action to stem over-grazing which threatens to destroy natural rangelands throughout a large area of the country. The report's executive summary emphasized the vital need to conserve rangeland, and under a sub-heading, *The Rangelands in Crisis*, the summary states:

The serious deterioration of the rangelands in Saudi Arabia has occurred over a long time. However, the degradation has accelerated recently and has now reached a critical stage where the problem is a threat to the nation's survival.

Until now the problem has seemed intractable; the creation of the NCWCD offers the first, and probably the last, opportunity to begin to redress this national crisis through the establishment of a national system of protected areas.

The grazing resources of the Kingdom have been stressed to the point of exhaustion with over 75% of the rangelands in a seriously degraded state.

The main causes are over-grazing and destructive fuel wood gathering. The rangelands cannot physically support the demands being made upon them by graziers with increasing numbers of stock and the resource is fast disappearing.

The problem has been acknowledged by the Government which addressed the plight of the Bedouins in the first three five-year plans which recognized the need to control grazing intensity and regulate range use. However, the fourth five-year plan is silent on the issue though range misuse has continued apace.

Saudi Arabia has an area of 210 million hectares with less than 1% suitable for arable agriculture – and, in the main, that is located over finite non-rechargeable aquifers.

Thus rangeland represents over 99% of the Kingdom and is the ultimate terrestrial resource for the salvation of its people in the post oil era.

Previously, Saudi Arabia was a net exporter of meat and animals. The situation is now reversed and domestically produced animals satisfy only 15% of the nation's growing demand for meat.

Saudi Arabia has established self-sufficiency in food as a strategic national goal, but despite massive government subsidies to the range livestock industry local production of meat has failed woefully to keep pace with demand.

205

The rangeland situation is a massive net-loss to the Kingdom. Not only is it sacrificing financial capital, but more seriously, it is causing a dangerous depletion of its environmental capital.

The major obstacle to resolving the massive problem has been the lack of focus for national action. That focus is now supplied by the protected area system plan being instituted by the Commission as this offers a suitable framework for action.

The NCWCD is committed to the conservation of biological resources within and outside protected areas. The success of these reserves will be measured in terms of the benefits accruing to people from the sustained production of biological resources.

This will only be achieved by instituting proper management systems for the reserves which necessarily involves the regulation of grazing. Thus the protected areas offer the Kingdom a timely opportunity to test and demonstrate sound resource use for the benefit of its people and to start the long process of regenerating its rangelands.

The protected area system is the key to sustained future prosperity of the nation – it must be made to succeed.

Much wildlife has been pushed to the margins of its habitats. The Farasan gazelle (*Gazella arabica*) was once widespread in the Tihama plain along the Red Sea coast of Saudi Arabia, but is now only found on the Farasan Islands. During our filming work in Arabia we were privileged to film this magnificent gazelle in its natural habitat. It is notably larger than other Arabian gazelles, bright red ochre in colour with an indistinct dark flank-stripe and a dark nose-spot. A healthy population is still found on the rugged terrain of the Farasans and several times we caught sight of them resting near the shoreline as we circled the islands in fast inflatable boats.

The Arabian guinea-fowl is another species which was once widespread on the Tihama plain but is now extremely limited in its distribution, occurring only in two valleys among the Asir foothills. Ornithologists regard the Arabian form as a separate race or sub-species of the helmeted or tufted guinea-fowl, *Numida meleagris*. Throughout its range in Africa the helmeted guinea-fowl has shown a marked decrease in numbers and the Arabian population is unique in that it enjoys the special protection of the community of farmers whose land it occupies. It is a sedentary, somewhat secretive bird, nesting on the ground in thick cover, and eating a wide range of items, especially seeds, shoots and cultivated grain. To combat the high mortality rate for eggs and chicks, they lay large clutches of up to 20 eggs and the young are self-feeding from a very early stage.

Plants are also threatened with extinction as a result of habitat destruction and increased desertification. Among the famed aromatic ancient produce of southern Arabia, myrrh featured prominently. The Saudi Arabian population of the myrrh plant (*Commiphora erythraea*) is now restricted to a tiny offshore island in the Farasan group, whilst a closely related species on the adjacent mainland is threatened by felling and grazing. The largest tree in Arabia, *Mimusops laurifolia*, is almost gone now with only 16 remaining at the last count and even these under threat. Other plants too are threatened with destruction whilst one or two have recently been added to the growing list of Arabia's extinct plant life.

Habitat reduction has affected many of Arabia's larger animals such as cheetah, leopard, gazelle, oryx, ibex, dugong, ostrich, houbaras and sea-turtles. In some cases the story of their existence in Arabia has been brought to the end of its final chapter. That sad finale has certainly come for the Arabian ostrich (*Struthio camelus*), a species which, like the houbara bustard, played a central role in Bedouin life for centuries. As recently as 100 years ago the Arabian ostrich was found throughout much of the peninsula. They were greatly valued by the Bedouin for their meat, oil, feathers and eggs. Hunted on horseback and killed by spear, or even the limited-range matchlock, they were fast runners and no easy target. There is a classic Nabati poem which extols the great speed of a courier's camel, comparing it to that of a fleeing ostrich: 'Hail, you rider on a speedy mount that runs like a terrified ostrich on level plains' . . . Respect for the ostrich as a difficult target is apparent.

What went wrong for the ostrich in Arabia? In 1989 in an article on birds of Saudi Arabia, ornithologist Michael Jennings summed up the demise of species quite succinctly:

> After the First World War, three things happened that tipped the balance very much against the ostrich: firstly, Arabia was flooded with modern rifles which could hit and kill an ostrich at a kilometre or more. Secondly, vehicles were used, particularly in the hard deserts of the north-east which were unfortunately also the preferred domain of the ostrich: cars used for hunting could effortlessly run down the ostrich, which previously had so easily outpaced the best of horses. Thirdly there was a much increased demand for ostrich plumes in the 1920s and 1930s . . .

Leopard and ibex are now found only in the most remote and rugged mountains of Arabia, and even there in greatly reduced numbers. Arabian oryx, as we shall see in the next chapter, have been issued with an eleventh-hour reprieve. The Arabian sand gazelle (*Gazella subgutturosa marica*) is a delightful animal particularly well adapted to life in stony or sandy deserts. It was once the most widespread gazelle in the whole of the peninsula, found virtually everywhere except in the mountains. Today it is on the verge of extinction, with captive breeding at NCWCD centres at Taif and Ath Thumamah likely to offer a last ditch attempt at reversing the downward trend.

In a recent NCWCD report on the status of Saudi Arabia's native mammals, Dr Iyad Nader lists 16 species which are now rare or endangered. This inventory includes nine carnivores and seven even-toed ungulates (artiodactyls). The report states that it is too late to include the Asiatic lion (*Panthera leo*) which vanished from Arabia just over a century ago. The last record of the Arabian cheetah (*Acinonyx jubatus*) is of two animals shot near Hail in 1973. (The cheetah survived among the mountains of Oman until recent times but its present status there is uncertain.) In addition to the Arabian sand gazelle, Saudi dorcas gazelle (*Gazella dorcas saudiya*) or *ifri* also is extinct in the wild in Saudi Arabia.

Habitat loss, combined with intense hunting, has also affected numbers of houbara bustard. Captive breeding is being carried out as a potential means to improve their status but, despite some impressive successes, considerable problems remain and environmental protection is still the first priority.

Urban growth and development have brought other problems for the Arabian environment. Apart from the spread across open land, pushing wildlife further and further away from traditional habitats, the cities create huge quantities of waste. City dumps, as in many other parts of the world, leave a great deal to be desired. Despite serious attempts to improve the situation wastes are often dumped in a quite haphazard manner with toxic chemicals mixed together with other refuse such as abattoir meat, construction debris and domestic rubbish. City dumps are often used as food sources for wild animals such as the steppe eagles and the hamadryas baboon, and this threatens to spread diseases among the wild populations of these animals.

The love of animals as pets has fuelled a new mini-industry in parts of Arabia in which endangered wild animals, both from Arabia and elsewhere, are stocked in cages. Not only does this cause suffering to the animals concerned and immense damage to the wild populations of captured species but escapee exotic pets have been inadvertently introduced to sensitive Arabian ecosystems, where they establish themselves at the expense of native wildlife.

In this chapter we have briefly considered the impacts of modernity on Arabia, reviewing the many advances made by Man and counterbalancing these against deprivations caused to nature, all in the name of progress. In our final chapter we shall see how efforts are being made to conserve the natural environment and how some species have been successfully rescued from the jaws of extinction, bred in captivity and re-introduced into the wild. Finally, we shall look at the way ahead and show how Arabian countries are demonstrating their determination to preserve as much as possible of Arabia's natural heritage.

Conserving

the

Future

The importance of Islamic attitudes to conservation in the arid lands of Africa, Arabia and Asia cannot be over-estimated since the vast majority of these lands are in areas where Islam is predominant. In Arabia, Islam has provided the roots for the present-day civilization and it guides the cultural values of all Muslims.

Arabia was not only the birthplace of Islam but the holy cities of Mecca and Medina remain the spiritual focus for the entire Muslim world. As many Muslim countries also look to Saudi Arabia and the Gulf countries for economic assistance, Arabian attitudes to conservation have global significance. Islamic teaching emphasizes that Man should live in harmony with nature and that the environment is under Man's care. In short, Man is the custodian of the natural world. A recent paper by Muslim scientists outlined five basic tenets of Islamic teaching with regard to nature: .

1   That man is a distinct part of the universe, whose elements are complimentary to one another in an integrated whole.

2   A relationship of meditation on, and consideration and contemplation of, the universe and what it contains.

3   A relationship of utilization, development and employment for Man's benefit and for the fulfilment of his interests.

4   A relationship of care and nurture, for Man's good works are not limited to the benefit of the human species, but rather extend to the benefit of all created beings and there is a reward in doing good to every living thing.

5   God's wisdom has ordained to grant human beings stewardship (*khilafah*) on the earth. Therefore in addition to being part of the earth and part of the universe, Man is also the executor of God's injunctions and commands. And, as such, he is only a mere manager of the earth and not a proprietor; a beneficiary and not a disposer or ordainer. For God alone

is the real owner of heaven and earth and all that they contain. Man has been granted stewardship to manage the earth in accordance with the purposes of its Creator: to utilize it for its benefit and for the benefit of other created beings, and for the fulfilment of his interest and of theirs. He is thus entrusted with its maintenance and care, and must use it as a trustee within the limits dictated by his trust.

(Dr Abou Bakr Ahmed Ba Kader and colleagues with Othman Llewellyn)

A traditional Arabian system of conservation which both predates Islam and is reinforced by Islamic belief is known as *hima*, whereby land was set aside for the common good in order to protect the grazing and wildlife species or to allow honey or wood production. The *hima* thus insured the survival of people in time of drought and the diversity of plant and animal life. *Hima* is an attitude rather than a specific set of constraints and varies from place to place. In Oman for instance, Bedouin in the Wahiba Sands withdraw their animals from the desert after rain in order to allow maximum growth. In other places, *hima* vegetation may only be cut by hand or grazing may be restricted to specific seasons. The largest number of *hima* are found in the more settled agricultural communities and it is in these traditional *himas* where botanists are today discovering many rare plant species no longer found in the surrounding countryside.

The prophet Muhammed who established new *hima* is known to have said: '*Hima* is only for God and his Prophet.' This statement has been interpreted as meaning that the governor of an Islamic state is allowed to protect the *hima* in the best interests of his people.

Drawing upon this historic experience, recognizing the need to change traditional attitudes into modern practice, the NCWCD in Saudi Arabia, assisted by the International Union for Conservation of Nature (IUCN) recently prepared a rationale document in support of a draft *hima* law. The proposed law 'provides for management of wildlife including the natural vegetation from protection to regulated use within prescribed *himas*'. The new system proposes five basic categories of *ahmia* (plural of *hima*) or protected areas, as follows:

1   *Strict Natural Ahmia:* for protection of key areas and ecological processes in which little or no consumptive use would be permitted. They would be managed by the NCWCD as 'bullion in the bank'.

2   *Natural Ahmia:* for protection of areas of national biological importance.

3   *Plant Ahmia:* for local protection of vegetation. Small, strategically located protected areas managed by local authorities.

4   *Resource Use Ahmia:* in which special care is taken to contain usage within sustainable levels.

5   *Hunting Ahmia:* for conservation of traditional hunting. Areas managed
in such a way that wildlife numbers are not reduced.

Whether future conservation administration follows this precise plan or
another similar one, there is no doubt that protected areas will feature as a
key element in the overall programme and that the *hima* system will be
revised and updated to meet current needs. The first major national park to
be established in Saudi Arabia was the Asir National Park. This encompasses
4500 square kilometres of mountainous terrain. The protected region is
highly scenic and of great scientific importance, containing many unique
and endangered species. A recent survey listed 34 mammals, 245 birds, 41
reptiles and 7 amphibians found within the park boundaries. National parks
have since been established in many other parts of the peninsula and the
protected area concept is now widely accepted as the best way forward.
Although in 1985 the United Nations List of National Parks and Protected
Areas noted only relatively small areas under protection in Arabia, there
are now considerable increases in protected areas for all the countries in
the peninsula.

Arabian countries are also experimenting with captive breeding programmes. In cases where environments have deteriorated too far or animal
numbers have fallen so low that natural breeding populations can no longer
be maintained, some members of the fast disappearing wild stock have been
captured and attempts have been made to breed them in captivity. The
most remarkable example is that of the Arabian oryx. Concern for the future
of this species provided the stimulus for an expedition, in 1962, to capture
some of the peninsula's last surviving oryx. Undertaken by the Fauna and
Flora Preservation Society in London in cooperation with the International
Union of Conservation of Nature (IUCN), Operation Oryx led to the
capture of two males and a female near Sana'a in Yemen. After quarantine
these three were shipped to Arizona's Phoenix Zoological Garden in the
USA to be joined by one female presented by the Zoological Society of
London, another female from Sheikh Jabir Abdullah Al-Sabah, Ruler of
Kuwait, and two pairs presented by the late King Faisal of Saudi Arabia.
Costs of transportation were met by the Shikar-Safari Club of Los Angeles
under the presidency of the late Maurice Machris, an ardent conservationist.

The original nine animals held in captivity in Arizona provided the
nucleus of a 'world herd' of Arabian oryx, the last wild Arabian oryx having
been shot in Saudi Arabia in 1972. Conditions for the captive breeding herd
were satisfactory and by 1978 the herd had grown sufficiently for animals
to be returned to Arabia. Initially, four animals were returned to the
Shaumari Reserve in Jordan, near Azraq oasis. They were joined shortly

after by two more females, and by several other animals from private herds held on the peninsula, re-establishing in Arabia a new breeding stock of the endemic oryx, by now extinct in the wild. Within ten years the Shaumari herd, held in a 22 square kilometre fenced enclosure, exceeded 60 oryx and other herds had been established at reserves in Bahrain, Qatar, Saudi Arabia, United Arab Emirates and Oman.

Having successfully re-established a viable gene-pool it was time to start planning the release of Arabian oryx back into the wild. Unfortunately there were few natural environments left in Arabia where released oryx could be assured of a safe passage. The first country to undertake cautious release of captive-bred oryx was Oman in 1980. Ten years later the wild population of Arabian oryx in Oman has almost reached 100 animals and prospects for a further increase now seem reasonably secure. Captive herds are increasing in size at all the Arabian reserves where they are currently held and valuable experience has been gained in husbandry of these desert mammals.

Zoologists involved with the Omani programme of re-introductions, however, remain highly cautious regarding its long-term prospects. They point out that things have not changed so dramatically since the days when hunting brought about extinction of Arabian oryx in the wild. It is virtually impossible to protect released animals from determined, well-armed marksmen and the only hope lies with strong education programmes leading to a change of attitude towards wildlife by local people. Such a programme has been operating in Oman since before the re-introduction of the oryx and it has made a strong impact.

The Arabian oryx, with its long, spear-like horns and conspicuous white body has become a symbol of modern conservation and provides the emblem for the Fauna and Flora Preservation Society. Its highly distinctive features are partially responsible for its sudden demise following the introduction of rifles. Unlike many desert animals it is actually conspicuous in the wild and can be seen from as far away as 4 kilometres, often standing on a slight rise, surveying the countryside. Biologists believe that this eye-catching behaviour is an adaptation enabling animals separated from the herd to be located and reunited with their fellows. But this, combined with the fact that they prefer to walk, rather than run, rendered the oryx an easy target for huntsmen with firearms and it is not surprising that it almost suffered the same fate as the Arabian ostrich.

The very features of desert adaptation which almost led to extinction of the oryx, act in its favour when it comes to captive breeding and re-introduction. Even captive bred animals have not lost the instincts for survival in the desert which their wild forbears possessed. They can still locate patches of isolated vegetation across miles of open sand by an acute sense of smell. Retaining a unique navigational capability, a solitary animal can recall the location of water drunk 12 months previously and trek 80 kilometres in a single night, following a direct route to the water and then back to the herd without erring from its course. The oryx's relatively benign nature ensures that they are easier to breed in captivity than some more fleet-footed gazelle. They are also able to eat almost all desert plants with impunity so, if necessary, the oryx can easily adapt to a new diet. Even the very conspicuousness which contributed to their downfall becomes a boon for monitoring surveillance of re-introduced animals. Unfortunately, few of Arabia's endangered species offer similar advantages in support of captive breeding programmes leading to re-introductions. Indeed, the success of Operation Oryx is now being seen as somewhat unique and not necessarily a precedent for the similar rescue of other endangered animals. Biologists stress that habitat preservation remains the priority for wildlife conservation and captive breeding programmes must remain only as a supportive method.

Recognition of the great importance of natural habitats has recently led to the establishment of many special reserves where remnant populations of endangered species such as Arabian sand gazelle, mountain gazelle, ibex and houbara bustard are still found. Many of these reserves are based upon traditional *hima* systems of conservation and marine parks are also under consideration with parts of the Red Sea already protected by bans placed on spear fishing and the killing of dugongs and turtles. The NCWCD has nominated 103 protected areas in Saudi Arabia including 56 terrestrial and 47 marine. It is envisaged that some 8 per cent of the Kingdom needs to be fully protected and managed if the full diversity of habitats is to be maintained.

While all of these measures will help to stem the tide of environmental deterioration and species extinction in Arabia, they will not be enough by themselves. Effective remedies must incorporate the management of hunting and the strict enforcement of hunting laws. There are simply too few animals to support mass hunting and there is ultimately little point in the enormous expense and effort involved in re-introduction programmes and the protection of a species from extinction if it remains in danger from sport hunters as soon as it steps, flies or swims outside a reserve.

The pressures of modern development on this wildlife heritage are now so great that many species will simply not survive without active protection, but it is not only a matter of isolated species. Whole regions are in danger of losing the botanical diversity upon which both man and wildlife depend. Unlike other lands within the great desert system of Africa and Asia, the countries of Arabia have small populations and the financial resources to

214

implement fully the protection of this heritage.

The challenge today is to find a new equilibrium that will balance modern demands with the creation of a new ecological order that reverses the present trends and preserves a great inheritance for future generations.

Further Reading

Agatharchides of Cnidus, *On the Erythraean Sea,* trans. and ed. Professor Stanley M. Burstein, Hakluyt Society, London.

Bindagji, Hussein Hamza, *Atlas of Sauda Arabia,* Oxford University Press.

Buttiker, Professor W. (ed.), *Wildlife in Arabia,* Stacey International, London.

Buttiker, Professor W., Krupp, Dr F. (eds.), *Fauna of Saudi Arabia* (Vols. 1–11), MEPA and NCWCD, Saudi Arabia.

Clayton, David and Wells, Keith, *Discovering Kuwait's Wildlife,* Fahad Al-Marzouk, Kuwait.

Collenette, Sheila, *Flowers of Saudi Arabia,* Scorpion Publishing, London.

Cornes, M. and C. D., *Wild Flowering Plants of Bahrain,* Immel Publishing Ltd, London.

Dickson, H. R. P., *The Arab of the Desert,* Unwin Hyman Ltd, London.

Dixon, Alexandra and Jones, David, *Conservation and Biology of Desert Antelopes,* Christopher Helm, London.

Edwards, A. J. and Head, S. M. (eds.), *Red Sea Environments Series,* Pergamon Press Ltd, London.

Fisher, W. B., *The Middle East: A Physical, Social and Regional Geography,* Methuen & Co. Ltd, London.

Gallagher, Michael and Woodcock, Martin W., *Birds of Oman,* Quartet Books, London.

Gauthier-Pilters, Hilde and Dagg, Anne Innes, *The Camel: Its Evolution, Ecology, Behaviour and Relationship with Man,* University of Chicago Press.

Hollom, P. A. D., Porter, R. F., Christensen, S. and Willis, I., *Birds of the Middle East & North Africa,* T. & A. D. Poyser.

Al Hout, Wasmir, *Insect Fauna of Kuwait,* University of Kuwait.

Jennings, Michael C., *Birds of the Arabian Gulf,* Allen & Unwin, London.

Jones, David A., *A Field Guide to the Seashores of Kuwait and the Arabian Gulf,* University of Kuwait.

Larsen, Torben, *Butterflies of Saudi Arabia and Its Neighbours,* Stacey International, London.

Lipscombe-Vincett, Betty A., *Animal Life in Saudi Arabia,* Garzanti Editore.

Nader, Dr Iyad, Abuzinada, Dr A. H. and Goriup, P., *Wildlife Conservation and Development in Saudi Arabia* (first symposium, Riyadh), NCWCD, Saudi Arabia.

Randall, Dr John E., *Red Sea Reef Fishes,* Immel Publishing Ltd, London.

Randall, Dr John E., *Sharks of Arabia,* Immel Publishing Ltd, London.

Schmid, Hagen and Vine, Dr Peter, *Red Sea Explorers,* Immel Publishing Ltd, London.

Schmid, Hagen and Vine, Dr Peter, *Saudi Arabian Red Sea,* Immel Publishing Ltd, London.

Sharabati, Doreen, *Red Sea Shells,* Routledge & Kegan Paul plc, London.

Silsby, Jill, *Inland Birds of Saudi Arabia,* Immel Publishing Ltd, London.

Thesiger, Wilfred, *Arabian Sands,* Penguin, London.

Thesiger, Wilfred, *The Marsh Arabs,* Penguin, London.

Vine, Dr Peter, *Pearls in Arabian Waters,* Immel Publishing Ltd, London.

Vine, Dr Peter, *The Red Sea,* Immel Publishing Ltd, London.

Vine, Dr Peter, *Red Sea Invertebrates,* Immel Publishing Ltd, London.

'Wahiba Sands Project 1985–7', *The Journal of Oman Studies,* Royal Geographic Society, Oman.

Walker, D. R. and Pittaway, A. R., *Insects of Eastern Arabia,* Macmillan, London.

217

Index of Latin Names

218

Index

Numbers in italic refer to illustrations.

221

Pictures

Jacket photograph The Telegraph Colour Library; insets, left & right M. McKinnon, centre P. Scoones

Inside

Page 33 Telegraph Colour Library; 34 N.W.R.C./A. Vareille; 34/5 M. McKinnon; 36 R. F. Porter; 37 M. McKinnon; 38 Ardea/G. K. Brown; 39 N.W.R.C. A. Vareille; 40 R. F. Porter; 41 top & bottom M. McKinnon; 42/3 B. Pambour; 43 Oxford Scientific Films/ M. Brown; 44 J. Grainger; 44/5 M. McKinnon; 46 N.W.R.C./S. Saustier; 46/7 M. Hill; 47 J. Grainger; 48 M. Hill; 81 J. Grainger; 82/3, 83 & 84/5 M. McKinnon; 86 T. Bomford; 86/7, 88 & 89 M. McKinnon; 90, 90/1 & 91 Planet Earth Pictures/Heap; 92/3 R. F. Porter; 93 Planet Earth Pictures/Neal; 94 Oxford Scientific Films/ Bartov; 94/5 M. McKinnon; 96 A. Kinneal; 129 J. Grainger; 130 P. Scoones; 131 Planet Earth Pictures/Scoones; 132/3 H. Schmidt; 134 & 134/5 P. Scoones; 136 & 137 P. Vine; 138/9 Planet Earth Pic-
tures/Pitkin; 139 P. Vine; 140, 141 top & bottom, 142 & 143 top & bottom P. Scoones; 144 left & right M. McKinnon; 177 R. F. Porter; 178/9 Robert Harding Picture Library/Jackson; 180 J. Grainger; 181 top M. Hill, bottom Oxford Scientific Films/Cooke; 182 M. McKinnon; 182/3 Planet Earth Pictures/Heap; 183 & 184 M. McKinnon; 185 top J. Grainger, bottom Bomford & Borrill; 186 & 187 M. Hill; 188/9 & 189 N.W.R.C./B. Pambour; 190 Ardea/G. K. Brown; 191 N.W.R.C./B. Pambour; 192 Ardea/G. K. Brown.

Text

We are grateful to the following for permission to reproduce extracts of copyright material: Curtis Brown for *Arabian Sands* by Wilfred Thesiger, 1959; Hakluyt Society for Agatharchides of Cnidus, *On the Erythraean Sea,* translated and edited by Professor Stanley M. Burstein, 1989; Unwin Hyman Ltd for *The Arab of the Desert* by H. R. P. Dickson, 1949.